The Golden Age

A Quantum Leap for Mankind

Tilakasiri Simon

PARTRIDGE
A Penguin Random House Company

To order additional copies of this book, contact
Toll Free 800 101 2657 (Singapore)
Toll Free 1 800 81 7340 (Malaysia)
orders.singapore@partridgepublishing.com

www.partridgepublishing.com/singapore

CONTENTS

ACKNOWLEDGEMENT

This book is dedicated to my loving parents,

Mr. U. D. Simon and Madam R. H. Somawatie

for being the harbingers of truth, which had a
great impact on me
during the formative years of my life.

I am deeply thankful to my dear wife,

D. Suchitra

for being a source of inspiration, a pillar of strength in my life and
for being there for me all the time.

Special thanks goes to

Mr. G. Kukananthan,

my friend and my mentor
who dedicated many precious hours of his life,
especially into the late hours of the night,
trying to help me to understand deeper truths of Life
and also for writing the FORWARD for this book.

Tilakasiri Simon

PREFACE

Dear readers, this book is written to give hope to humanity. Currently man is wallowing in the mire of problems of his own making. He is not to be blamed fully for the current situation he has created for himself. This is the result of the collective unconscious in the human psyche that has brought about the current situation man is in today. To add salt into the wound, man is being inundated with all kind of negative reports on a daily basis by the mass media so much so that it appears that the world is going to the dogs and mankind is doomed for good. We are being fed with half truths and lies, thus creating a negative perspective in our minds. This perspective does not at all augur well for anyone, given it is true that what mankind wants is to live in a peaceful world as a common brotherhood of man.

Man has created his own negative perspective of the world through the beliefs than he has been inundated with on a regular basis, and he holds onto it as the gospel truth. A lie uttered more often than not, will eventually be perceived as a truth on the long run. This perspective has to change and it must, and there are no two ways about it if we wish to bring about a new way of living, a more meaningful, a magnificent and an abundant life on this beautiful Mother Earth.

When we change our perspectives, we change the way we live our lives. This will bring about new experiences, more grander, more magnificent and more glorious than he can ever imagine. It is my hope and aspiration that this book will help to bring about *that* change in the minds of the readers, that shift in the individual consciousness, thus bringing about a quantum leap for mankind. This is the beginning of a new dawn. The Golden Age is at hand. Don't let it slip through. Most of all, don't miss it.

Tilakasiri Simon

FOREWORD

I have known Siri Simon for over 20 years. We have spent many hours discussing the big questions of living in an ever demanding world around us. As always, we ended up questioning personal intentions, values, beliefs and assumptions that may be presenting world views and related life challenges invited by these filters. What if the observer is both creating and attempting to figure out existence and his experience as an unconscious play of hide and seek? Are we, each one of us creating our individual worlds and also a shared world through collective professional, social and institutional consensus as we travel from cradle to grave? These questions would naturally emerge.

Our penetrating conversations never came to any absoluteness about living and succeeding in this world or about transcending it into any higher reality. But certainly it brought us to an openness that stimulated Siri Simon to look at a possible world from the other shore, regardless of what seems to be on this shore. Instead of dwelling on untangling our complicated world, can we, instead, invite a possibility that is free of having to bridge the past to the future?

Siri Simon says that unconditional love, inherent in our Being would do it. If only we allow that love to guide us, the New World

Order will unfold from the possible future into the present reality. As much as he draws upon the wisdom of Great Masters and leaders to get us to break free from the chains of the past, he brings out his own unique insights in ushering the New World into our consciousness. He hopes that, you the reader will notice that same seed that is sprouting in him is also nudging you from within, through the questions of your own life challenges and experience as it did for him.

Whilst all this may seem just wishful thinking, the personal changes in Siri's life confirms to him that there is a source of perfect order in us, and as we break through the crust of habitual thinking and feelings with powerful, original questions, this natural order begins to flow through our thinking and guide us forward quite magically, removing self-created obstacles as well. His experience outside of our dialogues, with various forms of healing systems corroborates that this is so. He has confirmed that there is a field of natural order-that it is the same unconditional love of our own natural Being that flows through in the healing of mind, body and soul.

In this book, Siri hopes to awaken the healing of the World— your world as well as the shared worlds with the conviction of his own realizations and experiences.

Mr. G. Kukananthan

THE GOLDEN AGE

A Quantum Leap for Mankind

"Only after the last tree has been cut down,
Only after the last river has been poisoned,
Only after the last fish has been caught,
Only then you will find that,
Money cannot be eaten."

-Cree Indian Prophesy

CHAPTER 1
A NEW WORLD ORDER

"By mind the world is led"
—The Buddha.

A New World Order is all about bringing about a new horizon, a new way of life, a life where greed and hatred have no place in our daily lives but only brotherly love, respect and understanding. It is all about restoring the self respect and the dignity of man. It is about giving people back to themselves through the process of raising the human consciousness above the current state of affairs.

Man has managed to tip the scales of balance and harmony, but unfortunately, not in his favor. Should no corrective measures are taken to restore the balance, we can all bid adieus and kiss each goodbye. This is because the larger System, of which planet Earth and man are part of it, will begin to restore the balance. The Universe is at all times trying to strike a balance. This balance is inherent in everything in the universe. Man is no exception. And in the process of doing so, Life as it is will have to make a change. The outcome from the natural act of balancing may not be something we may all desire. We may end up not existing at all and Life would have taken a different form all together. And this is all perfect as far as the System is concerned. Life adapts itself. Should we wish to continue life in the present state with all our achievements in all areas, then it is important that a shift in the consciousness of man be deliberately made. It has to be done consciously and it has to be done *now*. This is called Conscious Evolution.

"The cup is useful only when it is empty. With most of us, the mind is clouded, cluttered up with so many things. It is never empty. And creation can take place only in the mind that is totally empty. Creation is always new, and therefore the mind is made constantly fresh, young, innocent; it doesn't repeat, and therefore it doesn't create habits. To bring about

a different human being, and therefore a different society, a different world, there must be ending of sorrow; for it is only in the ending of sorrow that there is a new life."

—J. Krishnamurthi

RAISING THE HUMAN CONSCIOUSNESS

Raising the collective consciousness of mankind can take place when man as an individual raises his own consciousness. Whether we are aware of it or not, the human consciousness is constantly changing. Whether it is changing for the better or for the worse, positively or negatively, that is the crux of the issue here. To raise the human consciousness is to affect it positively and intentionally, with clarity, with precision and with focus, not leaving anything to chance.

What would be the purpose and the effect of raising the human consciousness? It would lead man to a global awareness, an understanding, a conviction, that man is not an island. He cannot be. Though he may be seen to be an individual but he is also the collective. He is a part of you and you are a part of him, and we are a part of the whole universe and most importantly, we are never apart and we will never be. This is not something new. Spiritual scientists of modern times and ancient seekers have spoken on this. They have been documented. Modern scientists are now coming to terms with these ancient truths. They are speaking of a Unified Field or a matrix that connects each and everything in this universe.

Man will realize that he is no more an individual making individual decisions as and when he likes. He will realize that his very thoughts about a decision he wants to take can cause ripples in the collective consciousness of man. This awareness will *shift* man's understanding about life as a whole and his position and roles in the common matrix. He will see a shift from his current modes of operations in his life to a level much higher where he can view himself as a co-creator of his outcomes of his life rather than a victim, as what he is experiencing right now. He would have moved from the *"I"* to the *"We"*.

Such a shift is already in the making. Many books have already been written with the hope that more and more people will awaken from their slumbers and start taking life seriously should we choose to continue life with all our achievements so far.

Man will come to realize that there are latent powers within him, at his disposal, which he now only wishes he has. It has been with him all this while but he has not been aware of it. Through the raising of the human consciousness, he will come to realize that we are indeed never separate from one another and that we are in fact just One appearing as many, existing at different rates of vibration and frequency and hence with different mindsets. Currently, we are creating situations through our actions and reactions, without being actually aware of the consequences of such actions. With indifference to the situations, we just go on and on in the mire of life, not knowing how to get out. Unknowingly, through our collective consciousness, we end up creating situations and circumstances that we actually despise.

The creation of a New World Order is about discovering new frontiers, quite alike to what Gene Roddenberry had proposed in his Star Trek movies, to venture into frontiers where no man has dared to venture before. This would be the most daring of all ventures of man, should he decide to undertake this mission. It is not an impossible task but at the same time it will be no easy task either. This journey has to be undertaken not by just a few of us. Many would prefer that the people in power and position like the politicians and the religionist, to whom we all look onto to solve our problems, would take the lead and all we do is just tag along, but it is a journey to be taken and explored by *all of us*. It involves everyone and it involves our life. This is a serious subject we are into. It involves everything that man has ever worked so hard for over the millennia. We just cannot afford to lose them especially the rich cultures of some societies, the multifarious languages, the music and the dances, the science and technology, the religions and spirituality and everything else that man holds onto very close to their hearts.

But then again, no matter how serious a subject can be, we just cannot afford to lose our sense of humor and lighten things up throughout our journey. As a matter of fact it is mandatory. And that's because we are 'light' onto ourselves. It is said that the lighter the luggage, the better is the journey. As we literally become 'light', we will tend to be less serious on survival matters but instead will soar high and enjoy the way we live our lives, together as one big family, from moment to moment. We will open our hearts and minds more and more, and in the process of doing so, we will become enlightened, ie we become light itself, our original state before we came into physical life. It is a state where all knowledge of the universe rests.

To venture into frontiers where no man has been, we cannot go there with our accumulated baggage and luggage in our minds. We ought to be new everyday of our lives, every hour, every minute and every moment. Every moment is a new moment and in every new moment is a new you and a new me. And to know this is very exhilarating and inspiring. There is much excitement around us, and within us.

But how have we accumulated this luggage? We have done so by listening to everyone else on this planet except to our own hearts. We have been listening to the politicians. We have been listening to the religious teachers for directions in our lives. We have been going from books to books, including all the religious scriptures for directions on how to live. We go to all the seminars the world would conduct to look for new ways and means on how we should lead our lives. Of course it is a good habit to read and understand many things from another's point of view. But mere reading books and listening to others just to past the time will only pass with time. This knowledge has to be applied in our lives for them to have meanings in our lives.

How important are all these knowledge? They are important to us as much as the warmth of the sunlight is important for the germination and the growth of a seed buried in the ground. All these knowledge should trigger in our minds for a deeper quest of who we really are. As long as this is not triggered, we will continue to delve into more and more books and attend more and more seminars, just to make ourselves feel good. And that is perfectly alright. We can bury ourselves with all the mountain of books in the world for all we want, no one will care. The fundamental question we must and ought to ask ourselves is:

> *"Have all these knowledge transformed me to be a peace loving person? Am I able to love another without any conditions?* And most of all, *"How have all this knowledge helped me to achieve the peace of mind and inner happiness that every living creature, from the lowest of the lowest worm to the richest king of kings, are looking for".*

If it hasn't, then why do we go on doing it? Now, supposing you are the captain of a ship and you are required to make a lone un-chartered journey and there isn't any form of reference as where to head and how to go. You are left without any guide. What would you do?

Simple.

You would have to do the most intelligent thing anyone else would do, that is, consult your own inner self. But however, when we are faced with difficulties in our lives, we do the most contradicting thing. We stop asking ourselves but instead look outward for others to give directions, look for others to tell us what to do and what not to do, we look into our Holy Books and see what our prophets have instructed us to do. By doing so, we have demonstrated a lack of self confidence in our own selves thus betraying ourselves by placing our trust and faith on another. We failed to realize that all those are only guides. The books, at best, are only guides. The teacher is a guide. The prophet is a guide. The Masters of the Universe are not here to make followers out of us but to make us masters of our own destiny. And the greatest Master will be the one who makes most masters out of his followers. Unfortunately the majority of the human population has taken the words in the books, the words of the teachers, the words of the prophets, the words of the Masters as *the* reality rather than the essence of what has been said. As such we have confined ourselves to a very limited way of seeing the world and the way we live and hence do not experience the freedom Life has to offer. Thus, we have failed the Masters who are living among us and the Masters who have walked the planet before us.

This is our lives we are talking about here. Why must someone outside you determine how you must live your live? At most they are mere guides. Of course there is no harm taking some cues from them now and then, but we have to remember always that they act only as guides. It is you who are living the life, not them. They have lived theirs and they are speaking from their experience. Their experiences *need not* be your experiences at all! A repetition of someone else's life is not called a living, but a 'copying'. The originality is not there, it is lost. Imitation robs the beauty of life. This is a serious matter as I said before. It is time to lighten the baggage and travel light. Only then we can hope to travel at the speed of light and 'be at all places at all times'. We have to summon all our faith in ourselves, our courage, our determination and our strengths, not just physical and mental strengths but more importantly our spiritual strength, because this is a spiritual journey we are into here.

Many of us have the mistaken notion that the politicians or the religionist will bring about a better world. At this moment of time and space, at the current stage of human development, it is not possible for them to do so. But eventually, once the spiritual problem is resolved, yes, their actions will propel the raising of the human consciousness to a higher plane, a plane of existence where no man has ever dreamt of. Their roles will come in later when the whole process is on auto-drive. There are many politicians and religionists with sincere intentions. Many of them have the vision and the sincerity of creating a better place to live in but at current stage, they will not be able to do it alone, in spite of all the available resources at hand. This is because the birth of a New World Order is in the hands of the *individuals*. The creation of a New World Order is an individual matter. World peace is an individual matter.

"Remember, your light shines through you when your light shines on another. The darkness of the world

can be illumined by your glowing presence—yet you must believe in yourself as The Source of that light and that love. All the world awaits your arrival today, shivering in its sadness, looking to you for warmth. Can you bring a radiance to those you touch today? Will you? Your answer will determine more for you than it will for them. In this is The Great Secret".

—*Neale Donald Walsch*
(Conversations With God)

The good news is we need not move a single step from where we are because this journey is not an external journey. It is a journey within, seeking who we really are. If we are but willing to take the journey, the journey within ourselves, we have taken the first step in the creation of a New World Order. It is possible only if we think it is possible. Everything is mind made.

Lao Tze said, *"A journey of a thousand miles begins with the first step"*. Are we courageous enough to say *"yes"* to the New World Order? If you say *'yes',* then the Universe is at your bidding. We must not doubt of what we can *be*. We have the ability to transform ourselves from a 1Watt 'bulb' to a 100Watts 'bulb' or maybe even a 1000W bulb.

When we come to an understanding of who we really are, that we are but spiritual beings undergoing human experiences in this magnificent journey of Light and Love, then we will understand each other better and will treat another better, with much respect, love and understanding.

Everyone is in a relationship with one another. In short, the creation of the New World Order is all about how we treat each other. It is all about creating new relationships, new ways of dealing with one another, new ways of interacting with one another, because the present ways do not seem to be working in providing man his peace and his happiness.

Man has been robbed of his peace of mind. The poor man is worried as to from where and when his next meal will come. The rich man is worried that his riches will be taken away. Both are constantly living in fear. This is not called 'living'. This is called existing in fear. So both men are constantly in mental agitation, never at peace. This is the reality of the world today. This is the order of the day.

There is a huge competition going on among men today. There is a struggle for power. Those in power are endowed with authority. There is a struggle to stay dominant. On our planet, the people or the country with the most wealth has power *over* others. And those in power will want to remain in power, and those who are not in power want to be in power. So power or authority equals money.

So in the process of attaining more and more money, to continue remaining in power or in the process of attaining power, we have thus created a world with unequal distribution of wealth. This has resulted in some people or countries having huge some of money, while other live on mere handouts. It is said that about four hundred million people die of starvation each day while at the same time, some others can afford to swim in fine champagne and have fine dining everyday. There are those who would fly a few thousand miles to a foreign country just to have a hair cut while others look so forlorn, not knowing where life is leading them to.

Certain industries, especcially the hotel industries, can afford to throw away food into their garbage bins while millions of children go to bed hungry every night.

The urge to stay dominant has not helped the majority of the population of the world. It has caused so much of hardship and sufferings, on a global scale. This *need not* happen. Our sheer greediness has pushed man to operate in a self-destructive mode. We can see very clearly that this thing called 'world hunger' is actually a myth. It should not exist in the first place as there is more than enough food for everyone.

> *"There is enough for everyone's needs*
> *but not for everyone's greed."*
>
> -*Mahatma Gandhi*

World hunger has been intentionally created by certain institutions just to stay in power. Let us just take the advertisement industry for instance. Billions and billions of dollars are pumped into that industry just on commercials, to get the products advertised. The advertisement boards, television commercials, cinema advertisement consume huge chunks of money. A small fraction of this money, if channeled to the hungry ones, will solve the so called world hunger overnight. Then what about the trillions of dollars that the countries spent yearly just on defense? Research on new artillery, new equipment and technology on military defense are done all in the name of staying in power. When will we ever wake up to the fact that that we are actually killing ourselves? We are blowing ourselves up. Is there a need for all these? Can we not feel our brother's pain?

Today, the whole planet earth is on the brink of a nuclear holocaust. Everything that we can set our eyes upon can be reduced to ashes. All it takes is one psychopath politician to get the fireball rolling and hey presto, it is fireworks everywhere. All our beautiful cultures, traditions and languages which we have built all these years will be gone. All the beautiful arts, architectures, natural landscapes, wild life will be gone. All the sports, poetry, songs and dances which we have created, will be gone. All family values, business ethics, sincere politics, medical marvels and the scientific discoveries will be gone. The various religions we have developed in worshipping God and Nature will be gone to ashes. In short, life as it is right now will cease to exist.

To avoid such a calamity, we need to take stock of our thoughts which are creating such a danger. Have we not suffered enough? Have we not seen enough of the cruelties? Do they serve us? Or do they serve anyone for that matter? Have we not seen enough wars? Do we need to experience more wars to wake up? Maybe these are all growing pains. We, man as a species, may not have matured yet. Perhaps we are still fighting like little kids. But if we are not careful, we can be wiped out for good. We cannot afford to be too careless. We have been careless for far too long. It is time to be responsible and stop the blame game and start behaving for goodness sake, for the good of all mankind, animals and the world at large. This will at least guarantee a better home for the children of the next generations to come. People of this generation can make that change if we are serious enough.

The question now is, *"Do we want to go on living like this and remain status quo, or shall we make a difference, first in our own selves and hence in the people with whom we come in contact with?"*

It is all up to us. Are we happy with the wars or do we need more wars? Are we happy seeing millions of fellow human beings dying of starvation? Are we happy with the human trafficking and the cruel ways little children are treated? Are we happy with all the cruelties, the insane and the ignoble ways of treating people, with genocides being committed by some insane despots? Are we? If we are not happy with the ways things are currently, let us take the bold step to make a difference. It is all up to us. We ought to make the decision. As Shakespeare would say, *"To be or not to be"*, it is all up to us.

The younger generation of people seems to be wiser than their parents. They can see what is going on. It is time the elders start paying attention to what the young minds of our society is trying to say, though the ways they express themselves may not be palatable. They can see through the hypocrisy of the elders as clear as daylight. They are telling us, in their own ways, *"Hey! Please stop it!"* They may rant and rave, shout and rebel, but let's listen to the essence of their message. This will hasten the birth of The Golden Age.

> *"It is definitely possible to bring about a totally new mind. But there are certain indications, certain necessary characteristics which do bring about that quality of newness. They are affection or love and integrity."*

> —J.Krishnamurthi

Philosopher and Spiritual Teacher, J.Krishnamurti

The present generation of people owe the children of this generation and the generations to come, an apology. An apology for the mess that we have collectively created. It would not be a wise idea to leave this mess to them to clean it up. We messed it up, we ought to clean it up for them. And for this to happen we need a 'revolution'. This revolution shall be a non-violent revolution unlike all the other political revolutions that saw bloodshed everywhere. This revolution shall be a *spiritual* revolution. It has to come from within. Because we have not gone *within* in search of our peace, we have instead looked into the outer world to bring about the changes. Consequently, we have created, not peace but 'pieces' everywhere. Our lives are in pieces. We have shattered dreams. The song is not over yet but we are going to our graves with the music still in our minds. How sad.

A revolution is a cry for freedom. It is an expression of the spirit of man, shouting out aloud, *"Hey, let me be free. I am sick and tired of all these unfairness and injustice."*

We as humans have been suppressed in every direction we turn to. Remember, we are a triune being. A being with a physical body, mind and spirit. The very fact of taking on a physical body is already a limiting effect on the spirit. It is already a difficult one. To make matters worse, we are given a whole list of dos and don'ts by our parents, the schools, the government, the politicians and the religionists, the very people to whom the masses look up to give them a sense of freedom. Religions would head the list of all suppressors of the feelings of human beings. Little wonder why many shun religions these days, especially the young ones. The young ones can clearly see the hypocrisy of the elders. The young minds are telling the elders to stop doing what they are doing to their fellow brothers. They are saying this in their own ways but their ways are not accepted by the norms of moral guidelines set up by the government and the religious teachers. It appears that all those in authority are self appointed moral policemen, telling others what they can do and what they cannot do, what they can eat and what they cannot eat, what they must wear and what they cannot wear, and in almost all other areas of living.

As mentioned earlier, it is already limiting for Life itself in the physical frame, and living a limited life has been more of a pressure than a pleasure. Living has been made narrow and more difficult by these moral policemen, telling us what to do and what not to do. So when all the avenues of expressions fail, and people cannot contain their frustrations and anger, there will definitely be a spill over. They have no other way but to express their feelings through a revolution. It is a way of venting their emotions and the ill-feelings in them. A brief study on all the past revolutions will reveal that people have been suppressed to an extent they no longer could tolerate. In this modern world of the twenty-first century, it is very surprising to note that in certain countries women folks are not treated equally with their male counterpart. They are treated like objects, to be used and then chucked aside. They fail to realize that women are also human beings with feelings, just like the men folks. They have been looked down, oppressed and suppressed in their homes and working environments.

We have to bear in mind that there is none superior to another. Just because the women folks appear weaker in physical strengths and smaller in size compared to their male counterparts, they cannot and should never be looked upon as inferior. This would in fact be an act of bullying. Women have other strengths which man do not possess at all. For example, their level of tolerance, their level of patience and the ability to express their love to their offspring is highly appreciated and commendable. The male counterpart is nowhere to this in comparison. This is only one aspect we are looking at and there are of course many others. Likewise, children are also abused in many ways. The young ones are telling us to listen to them. Is it such a difficult thing to listen to their little voices and their opinions? Are they not part of our community? Do they not have a right in what we do to the world? Of course they do. It is time we got everyone involved in decision making.

So, in the New World Order, everyone will be treated equally, immaterial of their country of origin, race, religion, skin color, gender, age or whatever differences there may be.

Let us all work together in the creation of a new world order. A world where *love* shall be the underlying principle of our lives. It is possible. It is all in our hands, in the hands of every one of us. Let the children of the world and the generations to come inherit a beautiful world. It is not too late. What is needed is a concerted effort from each and every one of us. Let it start with me . . . *"Let peace begin with me"*.

You may ask how the new world order will affect the lives of the people who come from a wide spectrum of beliefs, cultures, languages and nationalities and with all other wide diversities. The New World Order will take effect because man will begin to make a shift in the ways he views himself in relationship with his fellow brothers and also with the world. He would have changed his perspectives of the world. He would have brought about a shift in his consciousness, a positive shift, which would bring about a new paradigm, a new way of seeing and experiencing the world.

> *"If only people knew that they have the power to ask the Universe to change their reality, they would understand that they are not weak and helpless victims of circumstances, but empowered Children of Light exercising their birthright as Creator-Beings. A Being of Light is empowered to ask the Universe because the Universe is itself made of Light. So in a sense, when you send a signal out in the Universe, you are sending a signal into the essence of your own being, and it is because the Universe recognizes you as a Child of Light, as being one with itself in essence, that it obeys your request. Thus, manifesting a reality is fundamentally you and the Universe being as one, and moving as one, and this is the real secret of your own nature and your own power."*

—Beyond Limitations
—The Power of Conscious Co-Creation

The New World Order will see a new beginning in the affairs of the human beings at large including the animal kingdom, the natural resources, the vegetation, the ocean lives, in short the whole blue planet. It will see a new order of politics, parenting, education, commerce and religions.

When we understand that the need for a change in the human affairs is a great necessity, the *how* will be shown to us, without much effort. The 'why' must empower the 'how'?

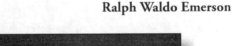

"Once you make a decision,
the Universe conspires to make it happen"

Ralph Waldo Emerson

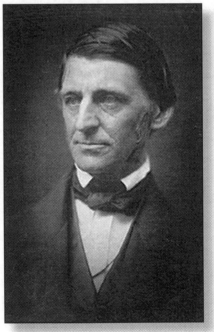

Ralph Waldo Emerson—essayist, lecturer, and poet

CHAPTER 2

COMING ANEW

"I tell you, I am in every flower, every rainbow, every star in the heavens, and everything in and on every planet rotating every star. I am the whisper of the wind, the warmth of your sun, the incredible individuality and the extraordinary perfection of every snowflake. I am the majesty of the soaring flight of eagles, and the innocence of the doe in the field; the courage of the lions, the wisdom of the ancient ones."

(Conversations with God, Book 3,
by Neale Donald Walsch)

What does it really mean to come anew? It is about stripping ourselves off all our layers and layers of personalities which we have wrapped ourselves up with from time immemorial. I don't know when we started to wrap ourselves with images of ourselves, which are actually of our own makings, but we ought to strip off all these layers and see our true self, and that is we are "nothingness" in reality. These images have given us a false identity of who we truly are, and unknowingly and unconsciously we have accepted these images to be who we are, and we defend and protect them at any cost. Now, do we see where all our problems have their roots in? It all begins with our false identities. There isn't a self in reality. If we can strip them off and be who we truly are, and that is being 'nothing' and no one in particular, we would have come face to face with an energy which is so freeing, so relaxing and so forgiving, which can radiate out from the centre of our being, and all animosities will just turn to dust. This is the state which we should be coming from at any given situation, for that energy will heal and neutralize any situations which are negative in nature. This 'nothing' is in reality the 'all thing' or the 'everything'. That is who we really are.

It is about living every waking moments of our life in optimism. This optimism is not a mind-driven agenda but a divinely inspired way of living. It is a state of mind where everything is possible because nothing is impossible for God. It is a mind saturated with the Divine energy and which fills every cell, every fiber, every molecule and every atom of our being. It is a 'place' of high self-confidence. Here, nothing can possibly go wrong. It is all well designed to the minutest detail and nothing is left to chance.

We have memories of the past. These self-images will just bring the past to the forefront of our minds whether we like it or not. Assume you had a bitter experience with your business partner many years ago. How will you act in his presence when you come face to face with him now, in this present moment? Would you come from the bitter experience and act from there? Would you go into another business deal with him again? If not, is it because of your past experience with him or you are not interested in that type of business at all. Assuming you do like the business opportunity, how would you respond to him?

Coming anew is not easy especially when we have unpleasant experiences of the past but the challenge is to take the bull by the horn and *create* things anew, immaterial of the past. If you had a misunderstanding with your spouse yesterday or last week, will you be resenting him or her? I doubt you would, unless it questions the integrity of the relationship. Otherwise you would accept your spouse as he or she is. The bottom line here is Love. How much are you willing to forgive another, whether they are our blood relations or not? If our ability to forgive is low, our acceptance of the person will be proportionately low. The reason we build mental walls around us is because of fear. Fear is the opposite polarity of Love. Because we choose to operate from a state of fear, we cannot come anew and break old barriers, which if broken can give us a whole new world of experience of what Love is. Fear has a crippling effect on our relationship with each other whereas Love provides a fertile ground for growth, for evolution of the human being to higher consciousness.

Coming anew at any given situation is an important criterion in our lives. And this is not easy especially when we are so accustomed to be led by the old mind. But the moment we see the futility of re-enacting the same old past which brings no happiness and peace of mind to anyone except heartaches, we will drop these old ways of thinking as how we would drop a red hot iron ball if we were to be holding one. Coming anew at any given situation is no easy task, but it is also not impossible. We tend to gravitate to our old ways of thinking but this benefits no one. This only creates separation and bloated egos.

To come anew, mindfulness of the situation helps a lot. If we do this constantly, it will become our normal way of living, sooner or later. Then you have helped to bring about the New World Order. For the New World Order to become a reality, it is of utmost importance that we come anew every moment. We do not have to operate from the current self-destructive mode which we are so used to. Thinking out of the box will give us a paradigm shift in the way we shall view the world and our lives.

In the days of The New World Order, every day would be a new day, every moment would be a new moment, and that is because we would be coming anew in every situation of our lives, without our past baggage. There would be no New Year resolutions but only new solutions to all our life situations, especially in our relationships with people. Love shall be the under-current. In the creation of a New World Order, we need not move a single step from where we are because this journey is a journey within, seeking who we really are. When we realize that we are but embodiments of Love, then we will understand another better. In short, the creation of the New World Order is all about how we treat each other in new ways because the present ways are not working in providing man peace and happiness.

Our thoughts have the power to impact our lives. But how we allow them to impact our lives, positively or negatively, depends entirely on us. Remember we can at any one moment choose to be creative or reactive. By being reactive, we will just be re-enacting our past. We need not do this. By being creative, we act from new thoughts. Every moment is a new moment. We can create a new you and a new me, immaterial of our past. The New World Order will not come to effect if we are stuck in the old mindsets. We must be serious in coming anew in every situation. The Universe is waiting in eagerness to respond to our actions. Suppressing others, especially the women folks, punishing others for their so-called 'wrong' actions, will not help the least. Remember, we have to come from Love and treat everyone alike.

We all may not be blood-related but we all are air-related. The air I breathe in is the same air that you breathe in. Only difference is in some places it is cleaner and in other places it could be more polluted, but air is air. There is no such thing as American air, Russian air, Indian air or Malaysian air. Of course we have Indian Airlines, but that's another topic altogether. This air is the one that makes our blood run through our bodies. Through this *one* common air, which is Life itself, we are *all* linked to each other. We are all each other's kith and kin. We are kindred spirits. We feel each others' pains and sufferings. We rejoice when others are happy. This shows our feeling of Oneness immaterial of all the sciences.

When we speak about treating everyone alike, it is not about equality as per se. It is about equality in opportunities. One's needs are not the same as another's. The needs of a family of five is different from that of a family of three. The basic needs of the former most naturally exceeds that of the latter. But then again if the latter is more qualified in a particular field and his/her contribution is more, then he is entitled for more things. According to his needs, he should be given. According to his ability to give, it should be taken and directed to other members of the society who are not so capable to earn and live a decent and a life of dignity, where his basic needs are well taken care of. Remember we are our brother's keeper and this maxim ought to be etched in our minds forever and ever. This idea will without a shadow of doubt, will erase greed from our minds. Greed, as it can be seen, is the chief cause of all these human miseries.

How about invasion and land acquisition? War is a big business. Can you imagine that? This has to stop. When the idea of Oneness is accepted, what is so wrong if we live together on the same land. Fairness must prevail. Leaders must at all times be fair to all. Social needs, religious needs and respect for each other's different practices must be accepted without any conditions. For us to grasp a fair idea of this Oneness factor, it may be necessary to understand a bit how we came to be where we are today.

In the beginning, there was only Love. And Love knows Itself. But Love knowing Itself was not sufficient. Love wants to experience Itself. And to experience Itself, Love has to be something other than Love, so that Love can be shared and hence experienced. Therefore Love manifested itself, in one holy sacred moment, from the One to the Many. We are indeed kindred *spirit*. We are truly One, all the time and no time. Now that it is many, it is still Love at the highest level. All the individuated parts are of the same quality of Love. For Love to experience greater Love, some parts have to know less about itself as Love. This was made possible through the process of forgetfulness. It was agreed that we forget who we really are when we take physical form, so that we can experience what we say we want to experience, ie. Greater Love. When the knowing and experiencing is blended, Love has then fully understood the true bliss of Love itself. Then the circle is complete.

With the understanding of this great Truth, we shall forever more rid our minds from the false belief that we are separate. We are not. We are but a true brotherhood of man. We shall stop, almost effortlessly, all the cruelties that we commit to another human being. This false 'I' or the ego will disappear and your true self, ie. Love and Light will shine through you onto another. Remember, we came here to do just that, to experience more and more Love.

CHAPTER 3
WE ARE ALL ONE

"We Are All One. Embrace this notion, make this the operating principle, overlay this on our politics, our economics, our religions, our education, and every area of our human society, and watch us create Heaven on Earth in one generation."

—Neale Donald Walsch

Jesus the Christ

The myth that *'we are separate from one another'* has created havoc in our lives. The truth is far from it. We are not separate beings although it appears to be so. We are from one source. This has been echoed in the major religions of the world. The book entitled, *"The Tao Of Physics"* explains this very clearly from the scientific point of view. Quantum physics are pointing to the matrix of inter-connectedness of the whole universe. The DNA or the building blocks of the whole Universe is in us. We are one with the Universe and with everyone and everything there is. The essence of all of us is not many but one. In short We Are All One. We are but individuated parts of the One Source. This essence can be called the Love energy. It goes further to explain that the whole world is within us, no, not the whole world *but* the whole universe is within us. We are but a microcosm of the majestic, colossal universe.

> *"All of Life, down to the tiniest cell, molecule or sub-molecular particle, contains intelligence. This basic intelligence is* **built in.** *It is a cellular encoding. Because that is true, these tiny particles move in ways that* **make sense.** *Their movement produces a specific and predictable outcome. This outcome is called Life. At the macro level, it is called the cosmology of the universe. At the micro level it is called particle physics, superstring theory and so forth. Some of you call this built in intelligence "survival instinct." All of your laws of physics and its predictability have been based on the understanding at which you just arrived.*
>
> *Now comes an interesting twist. At a certain point in the Process of Evolution, Life energy becomes aware that it is aware of itself. It is Life becoming*

aware of what LIFE IS in its present form. It is
supremely impacting because it produces what I
call the Separation Phenomenon. This is where an
element of Life first has the 'idea 'that it is separate
from God. It is the First Pivotal Moment. Prior to
this moment, energy particles expressed themselves
as part of an overall System. Their intelligence was
experienced as the intelligence of the System. In the
First Pivotal moment of self discovery, an energy
unit becomes conscious of Itself as a part of the
System, rather than the System Itself. Its identity as
part of the System soon expands into a thought that
it is separate from the System. This gives birth to
the next emerging process of Life called chaos. The
thought of being something "other" than the System
is what brings chaos to life. When a unit of energy
becomes self aware, it is losing its awareness of the
larger System of which it is a part. Its intelligence—
which is really the intelligence of the System—is
now experienced as its own intelligence. When an
energy unit sees itself as not part of the System, the
Life Form has created an illusion. It is the Illusion of
Disunity.

—Neale Donald Walsch
(Tomorrow's God)

This energy called Love is also known by several other names. Some call it the Universal Life Energy, the Universal Consciousness, God, Allah, Christ, Jehovah, Rama, Krishna, Spirit and a host of other names. But all these names represent the one common energy which is omnipresent. And this ocean of energy is in us, around us, above us and below us. We are a part of this energy, this complete, whole and harmonious energy. And it is a part of us. And the best part of this understanding is we are never apart, never had been and never will. This gives so much of assurance to us human beings. It gives us the feeling that we can never stray away for far too long how much it appears to be so, because eventually it will fall back to its original state. Nothing can possibly go 'wrong' in this universe. It is abundance onto itself. Our physical self is but a manifested form of this energy in accordance with the level of vibration determined by our thoughts. Thought are things, as we think so we become.

This being so, the essence of what we are or what we want is already here, in spirit. The spirit is who we really are. Without the spirit, we don't exist. In short, the spirit of you is . . . *you!* There isn't really a need. We all have been misled and taken for a ride by the religionists, the politicians, the economists and the capitalists, and most of all the mass media. They want us to be in the rat race and compete with one another and go for each other's throats at any cost. But it's not their faults. They have not come to an awareness that we, as a human race, are facing a *spiritual problem.* Once we set our spiritual issues right, our relationships with each other, the environment and the Universe at large will soar. Then all forms of agitations and the ugly way of living which we have been indulging in all these years, all these centuries, all these millennia, will eventually be phased out. Man will then be truly living. It is all about changing our perspectives. This is the beginning of the New World Order. It will be the dawn of the Golden Age. Not only man will rejoice, even the angels will.

The New World Order or the Golden Age need not be born after half the population of planet is wiped out by a thermo-nuclear holocaust. This must not and should not happen. For that to take place, man has to realize that no man is superior to another, irrespective of his skin color, his wealth, his race, the faith he professes and his nationality. Man has to come to an understanding that no sex is superior to another. A male is not superior to a female or vice-versa. Respect for each other is of paramount importance, immaterial whether that person is a male, female or gay. We shall then witness the true beauty of the diversities of life. It will truly be Unity in Diversity. No nation can claim it's superiority over another nation. No governments or religions can claim that they are better than the others, for they would have truly seen the truth. We would finally have come face to face with the universal truth, ie. *"We Are All One"*.

In the days of the new world order, man of different faiths will embrace each other as brothers. They will not see the existing differences as barriers and separate themselves but those very differences shall serve as unifying factors.

When this understanding dawns in the minds of men, we will all take responsibility for each other, immaterial whether they are our blood relations or not. The old selfish ways of thinking and acting will no longer govern our way of living. It will be governed by Love, kindness, generosity and a caring attitude. We will know that it is our duty and responsibility to help one another for we are all but kindred spirits, we are of the same kind. We shall be our brother's keeper.

> *"By birth is not one an outcast, by birth is not a Brahmin, By deeds is one an outcast, by deeds is one a Brahmin."*
>
> —The Buddha.

As a result of this understanding, no one have to live on the streets, in cardboard boxes anymore, children need not go to bed with hunger pangs anymore, wives need not lose their husbands in wars anymore, children need not lose their fathers in wars anymore.

In the days of the New World order, everyone will be taken care of, and there will be enough for everyone. Man need not lose their self respect and dignity. It shall be restored. He would have come to know of his Divine nature and hence he will walk without fear in his heart. He knows within him that he cannot be broken. It will be impossible to do so. He will then walk courageously with humility in his heart. There will be no arrogance, for there is nothing to be arrogant about.

It is a beautiful world right now itself only if we can accept what *is.* But we are so conditioned to reject what we don't like or want, and *only* look at what we like. By doing so we see only one aspect of life and not the whole of it. This creates conflict in our minds. Hence, we do not see the perfection of Life displaying itself in front of our own eyes, thus we complain, we cry, we curse and swear, rant and rave at Life itself. We will blame the God and the Devil, and everyone and everything in between. Oh! what a shame. To hasten the dawn of the New World Order in our daily lives, it is pertinent that we come to terms with all that has ever happened to us. Whatever is over, is over. Waste not another golden sacred moment in regret or guilt. Whatever has happened is for your own good, to serve you, to help you, in your growth in the solitary journey called Life.

Our current thought pattern has created the now existing divisions among man. The thoughts have created the thinker. The thinker happens to be the false 'I' which now dictates the mind of man. This 'I' does not exist in reality. Because of this 'I', we think we are different. As a result, we have separated ourselves, thinking that we are separate in reality. This is an illusion. But it is a perfect illusion. This illusion has a grand purpose. But man as a species, by thinking otherwise, has brought himself untold miseries.

We ought to know that it is by design that we have come to think of ourselves as separate beings. It is the natural process of moving from the knowing to the unknowing and back to the knowing again. When we take on a physical body, we have intended to forget our Divine union. This intention was done at the spiritual level. This agreement was agreed by one and all, so that together we can play our roles well. This forgetfulness is in a way a blessing. So, in reality, everyone is a spirit, an angel, a part of God, in disguise. We, as spiritual beings are undergoing human experiences in this magnificent journey of Life and of Love. Though we are a part of this whole cosmology, which some choose to call God, we are never apart. Even from the worst political despot who has the power to eliminate people from the face of this earth by the millions, to the most cruel rapists and murderers, there are messages for all of us. From the little innocent baby to the radiant monk in the caves, the crawling little worm, the tiny blade of grass, the pebbles by the sea and the rocky mountains, all have a purpose and sublime messages to all of us, through their way of life and existence.

Those who have eyes, will see and those who have ears, will hear of these messages. Here there is no right or wrong. Only our thinking makes it so. Each situation at hand has been called forth, and it has been delivered right on schedule. No event shall be called a misfortune. There is no such a thing as an accident or a coincidence. All events are perfect by themselves. They have been called forth by us, consciously or unconsciously, by our thoughts.

Therefore, all events are a form of blessing. Do not for once curse them. Just accept them, embrace them, be grateful to them and most of all, bless them. We just have to look for the hidden messages that come with them. It has come for a higher purpose. It is to remind us of what we have chosen to forget when we descended into physicality. It is to lead us the way to experience greater and greater Love. That is what we came to physicality for . . . to experience greater Love. But when we forget the purpose of us coming to physicality, we will curse all unfavorable conditions, thus making our journey a living hell.

But for mankind to accept this fact that We Are One and operate from this understanding and to accept it as a universal truth, this truth must first dawn into their minds. A wave of Consciousness has to sweep across the whole human psyche, igniting this little light of knowledge in their minds. This can happen when enough number of people can accept this truth and live by it in their daily lives. As Ken Keyes Jr. mentioned about the critical mass in his 'The Hundredth Monkey' theory, we too as a human race have to reach critical mass. And critical mass is reached when about 2% to 3% of the whole population commits to live by this truth. When critical mass is reached, it will sweep across the human consciousness like a tidal wave or a tsunami, creating a heightened awareness in man.

The Quantum Monkey
—The Hundredth Monkey Phenomenon.

In addition we find a journal article entitled "The 'Hundredth Monkey' and Humanity's Quest for Survival" (Stein 1983) and an article called "The Quantum Monkey" in a popular magazine (Science Digest 1981. Each relies on Watson as the sole source of information on the remarkable and supernatural behavior of primates.

The monkeys referred to are indeed remarkable. They are Japanese macaques (Macaca fuscata), which live in wild troops on several islands in Japan. They have been under observation for years.

During 1952 and 1953 the primatologists began "provisioning" the troops—providing them with such foods as sweet potatoes and wheat. The food was left in open areas, often on beaches. As a result of this new economy, the monkeys developed several innovative forms of behavior.

One of these was invented in 1953 by an 18-month-old female that the observers named "Imo." Imo was a member of the troop on Koshima island. She discovered that sand and grit could be removed from the sweet potatoes by washing them in a stream or in the ocean. Imo's playmates and her mother learned this trick from Imo, and it soon spread to other members of the troop. Unlike most food customs, this innovation was learned by older monkeys from younger ones. In most other matters the children learn from their parents. The potato-washing habit spread gradually, according to Watson, up until 1958. but in the fall on 1958 a remarkable event occurred on Koshima. This event formed the basis of the "Hundredth Monkey Phenomenon."

In the autumn of that year an unspecified number of monkeys on Koshima were washing sweet potatoes in the sea. Let us say, for argument's sake, that the number was ninety-nine and that at eleven o'clock on a Tuesday morning, one further convert was added to the fold in the usual way. But the addition of the hundredth monkey apparently carried the number across some sort of threshold, pushing it through a kind of critical mass, because by that evening almost everyone was doing it. Not only that, but the habit seems to have jumped natural barriers and to have appeared spontaneously, like glycerine crystals in sealed laboratory jars, in colonies on other islands and on the mainland in a troop at Takasakiyama.

A New World will come about when a new you and a new me is born. Every moment is a new moment. We can create ourselves anew at any moment we want. We need not stick to the old ways, knowing very well that they are not working the way we say it should. It has nothing to do about being right or wrong. We need a paradigm shift. We have to come out of this paradigm of being right or wrong. It doesn't have to be this *or* that. It can be both.

If it stands stark nakedly in front of us and shows us that the current ways of living are not working for us, not providing the ways and means in giving us more peace and more love, more of what life has to offer from the universal abundance available, we should start asking ourselves why are we still doing what we are doing. If our politics are failing us, then we should change what is not working for us. If our religions are failing us, we ought to look into them in new light and see what could be the stumbling blocks that are preventing us from experiencing harmony and unity. At the present moment of time and space, our politics, our religions, our business ethics and our science are killing us, tearing us apart.

A new you and a new me is 'born' when we embark on new ways of thinking and new ways of looking at the way we are living our lives. We will not only revamp our politics but also our ways of doing business and also our religions. We will revamp our education system and will take a deep look at the ways we run our families, the way of upbringing our little ones and the way we care for the animals, the environment and planet Earth at large.

This brings us to the topic of relationships. Relationship is everything in life. It is only through our relationships with the outside world that we can find ourselves. Escaping to the forest or into the caves seeking solitary living will be a futile effort. We can afford to lose many things in the course of living our lives, but make sure we never ever lose our sense of humor. It is a fine ingredient for a harmonious relationship with one and all. In the days of The New World Order, there will be no 'rotten apples.' There will only be people who may not share your opinions or views. That does not warrant us to brand them as rotten apples. They too are human beings with feelings. They too are children of God. No one does anything "wrong" given the model of the world they hold in their minds. It is important that in all our dealings with every member of the society we live in, we ought to come from a compassionate heart. Clashing of our egos will bring no benefit to anyone. It only boosts our egos. And we shall always want to remain 'right' and try to prove the other 'wrong'. Of what use are all these? All shall be in vain. It would do all of us a great favor if we but choose to remember the Golden Rule of Life as stated by Confucius.

"Do onto others what you would want others to do onto you."

In any event of an argument or in a time of extreme anger, all we have to do is just ask a simple question, and that is, *"Who am I?"* In that very moment, a different kind of energy will arise and you will find out that the anger will dissipate and you will not resort to abuse another either verbally or physically, or both. It is the belief in the existence of a false self that is tormenting us, day in, day out. That false self is our ego.

> *"The fool who does evil to a man who is good, to a man who is pure and free from sin, the evil returns to him like dust thrown against the wind"*

> —*The Buddha*

In the days of The New World Order, man will come to a realization that he cannot possibly short-change another, cheat or lie to another. This is because he would have realized that the consequences of the impact of such negative thoughts that befall him would be of more malevolent than benevolent. Such an act is only possible when we come from the old mind which says that we are separate and that we need to compete for survival. But this is not possible when we come from the understanding that We Are One.

> *You often say, "I would give but only to the deserving," But the trees in your orchard say not so, nor the flocks in your pasture. They give that they may live, for to withhold is to perish. Surely he who is worthy to receive his days and his nights, is worthy of all else from you.*

> -Kahlil Gibran

Let our lives be like a Stream of Love, wandering freely without any prejudices and discrimination. Touch the hearts of each and everyone who comes in contact with us with equality and fairness. Living thus, we are expressing our true nature, and our true nature is Love itself. Touch their hearts, not just our close kith and kin but anyone that comes our way. We will come to realize that we are all but one big family. Man is truly magnanimous. He is but the embodiment of Love.

> *"Can a blind man lead another blind man? Will they not both fall into a pit? Why do you see the speck in your brother's eye, but not the log that is in your own eye?*

> —Jesus Christ

In the days of the New World Order, man will not seek to find the specks in his brother's eyes as he would have known that there is a log in his. When his own vision is blurred, how could he see the perfection in others. He would first seek to remove the log from his own eyes. In the days of The New World Order, man will demonstrate his magnanimity by his ability to embrace his worst 'enemy'. His will forgive and forget ever more willingly for there is nothing to hold back his Love for others. Man ought to see that there is only One God, and He is omnipresent. This understanding will bring about a brotherhood of man. In the New World Order, people of different races, different nationalities, different religious backgrounds, who speak different languages, will come to a common platform of brotherhood. The Race of Humanity shall outshine all other varying races. The days of The New World Order will truly be of the Golden Age. In the days of The New World Order, man will no more operate in the paradigm of right and wrong. Man will not try to prove himself right and the other wrong. He would work from the paradigm of *"what works"* and *"what doesn't"*. He would have realized that it doesn't pay to prove another wrong. We are magnificent beings. In the days of the New World Order we will express this magnificence by not allowing children to die out of starvation and by not killing people just because they disagree with us. We will leave behind these primitive ways of living, and instead embrace each other like brothers and sisters.

Remember, we are our brother's keepers. In the days of The New World Order, we shall live simply so that others will simply live. Everyone can live a life of dignity, and that is because we made it happen by reinforcing the principle of Oneness in our daily living. When we hurt another, we will feel the remorse when the emotions die down. This clearly shows that there is only one of us all the time. When we come to this wisdom, that We Are All One, we will put an end to all kinds of abuse and mistreatment of another. We will stop hurting another. We shall embrace another as our own, for in reality, there is no another.

Not only that. We shall help, care and share to uplift his self confidence and self dignity. This we will do not because our prophets said so or not because our Holy Books said so. We will do it because we are kindred beings, we *feel* for each other because we are connected as One. We are from the same Source.

In the days of The New World Order, the family unit will no more be confined to what it represents today. The family unit will be from a larger circle of people which includes the whole community. We will extend our love and care to members of the community as if they are our own. The current sense of ownership of 'my spouse' and 'my children' will be something of the past. Remember, We Are All One.

The old selfish way of thinking and acting will no longer govern our way of living. It will be governed by Love, kindness, generosity and a caring attitude. We will know that it is our duty and responsibility to help one another. In the days of The New World Order, man will realize that it is really futile to spend trillions of dollars on arsenal build-up, in the hope of maintaining 'peace' among nations. It is far better to build a beautiful character that would ensure lasting and genuine peace and harmony, pervading the entire world, for when there is beauty in character, there will be harmony in the homes all the world around.

CHAPTER 4

THE SACREDNESS OF LIFE

"The conditions with which you meet in the world without are invariably the result of the conditions obtaining in the world within, therefore it follows with scientific accuracy that by holding the perfect ideal in the mind you can bring about ideal conditions in your environment."

—*Charles F. Haanel*
—*The Master Key System*

Khalil Gibran—artist, poet & writer

Can we be sensitive to the pains and sufferings of other human beings? Can we be sensitive to the pains and sufferings of the animals? If we can be sensitive enough, we will not kill another human being no matter whatever the reasons may be. We will not slaughter another animal, for food, for sports, for amusement or even for medical advancement. That is because Life is sacred and Life is meant to be preserved, not destroyed.

Life has to be revered. Life is but an expression of the Divine Energy. This energy is magnificent by its very nature. And this magnificence is present in everything in this whole Universe. This energy is the same as it is in the rocks, as it is in the worm as it is in the humans. All are but manifestations of the Life Energy. This life energy is pulsating in the rocks, it is moving in the plants, it is self-aware in the animals and it is aware that it is self-aware in the humans. All has a role to play to ensure the succession of this life principle and therefore no life aspect is less important than the other. It is of utmost importance that life be revered and for that Life has to be preserved, ie pre-served, served before serving anything else. Unfortunately today, life is taken for granted. Life forms are being destroyed and abused at a grand scale. For example the rate of destruction of the tropical rain forest throughout the world has led to the destruction of habitats of various species resulting in the extinction of thousands of plant and animal.

I am not talking just about plants and animal life but also that of the humans.

We are in the twenty first century and we do know the inter-dependence of all life forms on each other. Hundreds of books have been written on this global issue. Hundreds of NGOs have made their appeals on this matter but in the earlier years all these fell on deaf ears. Lately there are some signs among certain governments who have been seen to have awakened to their ideas and their cries. Majority still don't care a hoot and they do not seem to be stopping or even slowing down. Is our daily newspaper more important than oxygen?

Do we not realize that the oxygen we breathe is dependent on the trees around us, which in turn need the carbon dioxide for their survival, for the process of photosynthesis? Of course we do. And yet we still contribute to our daily newspaper, which by the way brings more depressing and horrible news than the good news. Isn't there any other way of getting our daily news, other than the newspaper? Can we imagine the numbers of trees we **need not** cut down if we just stop printing newspapers? Of course there are other means of getting the news, like the internet. But the newspapers are so profit-oriented that the owners do not seem to care a bit on its impact on the world at large.

Not only the news can be depressing but the oxygen level on the whole planet is depleting and this adds to the already existing depression. This will eventually cause planet Earth to make its natural shift to make up for the imbalance which man has created, just out of sheer greed. Animals are not spared either. The amount of animals that are being slaughtered on a daily basis for human consumption is very alarming. The amount of blood that flows daily from the slaughtering of these poor innocent animals can overflow the banks of Ganges River. Have we ever been to a slaughter house to see and hear the cries of the dying animals? When we cannot even show a little compassion to our fellow humans, and we kill them with impunity in the name of religions, in the name of a God or the Devil, in the name of nationalism, what more to speak about compassion to animals.

This is a very sad state. Have we evolved to be so feeling-less towards other life forms. Can we not feel their pains and sufferings? Man is not a robot. But he has made one out of himself. This has not even stopped him from mistreating his fellow humans, leave alone the plants and animals. We have built sophisticated weapons just to kill our fellow brothers. If we are being attacked by some unfriendly aliens from outer space, then at least we can justify the trillions of dollars spent on defense every year, but we are not fighting any aliens. We have been fighting among ourselves! And all the sophisticated weapons are designed and built just to kill and destroy fellow humans, in larger numbers.

Do we not feel the pains in the hearts of the mothers, the husbands and the children whose son or wife or father who has been killed in a war? With the deep sadness in their hearts, they will have to continue with their lives. Is it necessary to live like that? Do we not have other options? In the name of nationalism and patriotism, we march thousands and thousands of young men and women across the battlefields, telling them it is their duty to defend the country. In such a cause, millions and millions of human beings, civilians and soldiers are deprived of their lives. When are we ever going to say to ourselves and say enough is enough?

> *"Whoever kills another one without justifiable cause, surely he is killing all of humanity. And whoever saves the lives of another, surely he saves the lives of all humanity."*

> —Sura Al Ma'aidah:
> Ayah 32 (The Holy Quran)

There is too much of sadness and sorrow in the collective human psyche. I think it is time we heal these energy fields through Love. Love is the only solution. Have we seen how the rich and powerful use the poor and the weak for their benefits? Although we do not hear of slavery these days, modern man is far more worse off than the slaves of those days. He is being abused and abused till his bone breaks. Look at the number of child laborers. The wealthy do not seem to care from whom they can get their services from, as long as they get to enrich themselves, weather it is from the children, the women or the men or even the animals, they do not care a wee bit. What is important is that their bank account must grow at any cost. Greed is *the* factor for the downfall of man. We seem to be more interested in superficial things around us.

Have we ever paused for a moment to watch a bird in flight, the leaves and branches of a tree swaying in the winds? Have we ever caressed a kitten or a puppy and put it to our face, or look into its eye and see the innocence and their beauty of their little souls. Have we ever stopped by a flower, just to observe its beauty or to smell its fragrance? There is beauty around us but we do not see.

In the days of the New World Order, man will continue to have different opinions and views with regards to matters relating to the political climates, the economics of the country, the education systems and all other affairs. But man will not kill each other over the differences in opinions as he is doing right now. That is because he has understood that Life is precious and has to be preserved. Wanton destruction of lives, be they of humans, animals or vegetation, will be something of the past. Man would have so evolved that he would have come to a state of mind where is very conscious and attentive to his environment. His awareness on the impact his /her actions would have on the environment would be a heightened one. There would be no room for carelessness. Whatever that needs to be done will first be felt intuitively.

> *"Treat the Earth well; it was not given to you by your parents, it was loaned to you by your children. We do not inherit the Earth from our ancestors; we borrow it from our children."*

> **—Native American Indian Proverb**

CHAPTER 5
SIMPLE LIVING

"Live simply so that others can simply live"

-Mother Teresa

Mother Teresa

Living simply can be the greatest boon to all mankind and also to the world at large. Nowadays man is caught up in the race to acquire more and more, thinking that the more he has, the happier he will be. This is a myth. Unfortunately this myth has become the order of the day and has robbed man of his inner peace and happiness.

> *"Wealth have I; Sons have I; Thus a fool thinks;*
> *When he himself is not his; What more to speak of*
> *sons and wealth"*

—The Buddha

In the days of The New World Order, man will no more grab so that others will grief. He will give away even his priceless possession for he would have known that to possess is a lie. Whatever he gives away, he is only giving onto himself, for there is only *one* of us all the time. For all his giving, the Universe will bless him a thousand folds. It will truly be a bountiful harvest for whatever that is given is never lost. Simple life does not consist in the mere possession of a few things but in the freedom from possession and non-possession, in the indifference to things that comes with deep understanding. Merely to renounce things in order to reach greater happiness, greater joy that is promised, is to seek reward which limits thought and prevents it from flowering and discovering reality. To control thought-feeling for a greater reward, for a greater result, is to make it petty, ignorant and sorrowful.

Simplicity of life comes with inner richness, with inward freedom from craving, with freedom from acquisitiveness, from addiction, from distraction. From this simple life there comes that necessary one pointedness which is not the outcome of self-enclosing concentration but of extensional awareness and meditative understanding. Grabbing for ourselves will cause others to grief. This will snowball from personal emotional imbalance within to social imbalance without. The Universe is Abundance itself. We are a part of the abundant Universe. There is enough for everyone. We have to call forth what we already have, in the spiritual realm, to physical manifestation. Always remember, we are complete spiritual beings undergoing a physical experience. The Universe will bless the giver with a thousand folds because the Universe will detect the sincere thought of giving in the giver as both are in communion all the time. The giver is not apart from the Universe but will always remain a part of the abundant Universe. So when we give, come from the state of abundance and not from a scarcity mentality.

Simple life is not the result of outward circumstances; contentment with little comes with the riches of inward understanding. If you depend on circumstances to make you satisfied with life then you will create misery and chaos, for then you are a plaything of environment, and it is only when circumstances are transcended through understanding that there is order and clarity. To be constantly aware of the process of acquisitiveness, of addiction, of distraction, brings freedom from them and so there is a true and simple life.

But the New World Order will not just happen. A new world order will not just fall from the heavens Just as we have created this current world order, of which many are not too happy about it by the way, the New World Order too will have to be created. The human race has collectively created the mess we are in now. People can be categorized under two beliefs system as far as the economic cake is concerned. Majority of the people are of the mindset that the things they need in this world are fixed. As a result of this mindset, they will compete at any cost to get the most. This has resulted in some having more and some having little or none at all. This is the reactive mindset. It is the *"survival of the fittest"* mentality. And we are killing ourselves. Then we have a small group of people who have the mindset that we can *create* the economic pie to whatever size we want to. This is the creative mindset. In this situation, all types of mental and physical tensions will disappear. We do not have to deprive the others in the process of getting what we want in life. In this manner, we immediately rid of our minds all forms of envy, jealousy, tension and a host of other social issues which man is facing today. We will come to the understanding that all these need not necessarily be part of our lives.

A new world order will take birth when we rid our minds of such myths which we have been adhering to for a long time. *'Survival of the fittest'* is such a myth. It applies to the animal world perfectly. But man is more than an animal. The belief in the 'survival of the fittest' implies that there is not enough for all of us. So we ought to grab and hoard at any cost. This thinking pattern has brought about the current *"dog eat dog"* world, causing much misery to mankind, including all the wars. We need not live our lives these ways. There are other ways. These miseries are not the work of a devil or a God, as many would conveniently like to shift the blame to. We have to take responsibility for all these makings.

All is not lost. The good news is we have the tools and the ability to undo it. It is all what we intend to *be*. If the present situation is not in our favor, in the creation of a brotherhood of man, then why do we go on creating it again and again, by our thoughts and actions? Let us change the way we *think* and hence bring about a new world order. It will be almost effortless. We have to make The New World Order a reality. Mere wishing will not do. It won't just happen and it won't happen in a year or two. It may take a decade or two, or maybe even a generation. But then who is counting? It really doesn't matter as long as we are willing to take the first step. Our thoughts have the power to impact our lives. How we allow them to impact our lives, positively or negatively, depends entirely on us.

The dog-eat dog world of ours is about grabbing as much as we can for our own benefit and also for the benefit of our loved ones, which may include our immediate family members, and that's it. The rest can go to hell for all we care. That is the current operating mode of the human minds. As long as I have enough for myself and as long as I can hoard as much as I can, for the "rainy days", it is perfectly alright. My neighbors can starve to death for all I care. It is their darn problem. If I can work hard why can't they. It is all because of their innate laziness. Such ways of thinking has not really helped man as a whole. This is because we have been taught that we are separate.

We have been taught that we are not only *separate from each other* but we are also separate from the Universe, we are also separate from God. We are taught that we individuals and we have to seek ways and means for survival. If you don't help yourself, no one else will. This has brought about the unhealthy competitive world we live in. This has resulted in a small group of the population having most of the wealth, while the masses suffer. Grabbing for ourselves has caused others to grief and to suffer. This has snowballed from personal emotional imbalance within to social imbalance without.

Many social problems have resulted from this kind of thinking and acting. People are caught up with the idea of ownership. A document to say that they own a house, a car, a piece of land, a bank account, is sufficient to make them feel happy. It is just a document, a piece of paper. With this kind of scarcity mentality, we have opted to disown the abundant universe. So with this kind of mentality we have brought about great misery and unhappiness to many people in the world. This is our selfish nature *in action*. Let me show you one of the side effects which we have brought about onto our fellow brothers and sisters. It is called World Hunger. The world's hunger is getting more and more ridiculous by the days. There are more fruits in a rich man's shampoo than on a poor man's plate.

World Hunger

Hunger is the feeling one experience with a lack of food, the "persistent gnawing condition resulting from a lack of adequate food intake, which prevents one from working or thinking correctly." Starvation is the most severe case of the condition of hunger. Starvation and hunger, if not combated, lead certainly to malnutrition. Malnutrition is the condition resulting from a lack of life sustaining vitamins, minerals, proteins, fats, and carbohydrates.

Furthermore, malnutrition slows the intellectual development of children and young adults, and therefore, the problems of hunger and disease in third world countries cannot be solved internally but need outside influence and aid. The UN and other world hunger organizations offer significant economic and medical aid to these countries to help stamp out hunger.

Hunger is not a problem because the world food production is not enough to feed all of the people in the world; it is a problem because the food is not distributed equally among all of the countries and people in the world. Third world countries that have a great percentage of the population starving do not have the resources to obtain or grow food. These countries also have a lower standard of living than second or first world countries, as well as a non-existent economic infrastructure, or if one does exist, it is unstable. These factors also have an impact on a country's technological capabilities. If all the food in the world were divided equally among all the people in the world, each person would get three times the minimum amount needed to survive. If there was a feasible way to accomplish this enormous task, the solution to world hunger would be found. Until then, charities and donations must aid the organizational fight against world hunger.

SOME STATISTICS ON WORLD HUNGER

Every 3.6 second someone dies of hunger.

Every year 15 million children die of hunger.

One in twelve people worldwide is malnourished, including 160 million children under the age of five.

Nearly one in four people, 1.3 billion total, lives on less than US$1 per day.

One out of every eight children under twelve in the US goes to bed hungry every night.

Half of all children under age five in South Asia and one third of those in sub-Saharan Africa are malnourished.

To satisfy the world's sanitation and food requirements would cost only UD$13 billion— *what the people of the United States and the European Union spend on perfume each year.*

Some 800 million people in the world suffer from hunger and malnutrition, about 1000 times as many as those who actually die from it each year.

South Asia has the largest number of poor people (522 million of whom live on less than the equivalent of US$1 a day.) Sub-Saharan Africa has the highest proportion of people who are poor, with poverty affecting 46.3 percent or close to half the region's population.

Nearly 1 billion people are illiterate; more than 1 billion people do not have access to safe water; some 840 million people go hungry or face food insecurity; about one-third of all children below five years old suffer from malnutrition.

The estimated cost of providing universal access to basic social services and transfers to alleviate income poverty is between US$50 to 80 billion, which is less than 0.5 percent of global income.

The top fifth (20 percent) of the world's people who live in the highest income countries have access to 86 percent of world gross domestic product (GDP). The bottom fifth, in the poorest countries, has about one percent.

The assets of the world's three riches man exceeded the combined Gross Domestic Products of the world's 48 poorest countries.

Source: www.thehungersite.com
Posted by Jonathan Crabtree at Labels.

GETTING OUT OF THE VICIOUS CYCLE

The poor man on the street will have no time for philosophy. He may not even have time for God. His immediate issue is to find food to fill his stomach. Once his hunger is satisfied, then we can talk all kinds of philosophies to him. As long as he is always in a state of want he will be always be in a state of discontent. Constant craving is the cause of un-satisfactoriness. As long as man is always in a state of wanting, he will continue to experience that state, that is, a state of lack. And this is because a state of wanting makes the universe push away the very things you want.

Our thoughts of wanting is the signal we have sent to the universe and it will respond to our request. As such, we will find ourselves caught in the vicious circle over and over and there is no sight of getting out of it. A man is poor not because he likes to be poor. A man is poor because he has been made to be poor by intention, by those who are well to do. He has been robbed 'psychologically'. So, psychologically he is always looking for ways and means to fulfill his immediate wants and needs. His psychological issue has created a physical problem, that doesn't seem to have a light at the end of the tunnel.

This is the kind of mentality that has impoverished man. It makes him feel poor and thus he thinks he is poor and will feel poor and as a result, he will experience poverty. This vicious cycle must stop. We need not be the owner to just a concrete building, or a car, or a piece of land. We can claim our kinship with the whole of nature, the mountains, the rivers, the oceans, the vast sky and the infinite universe. And see for ourselves how our mind expands. See how magnanimous we are. If we can often come from such a state of mind, we are in fact experiencing abundance all the time. There is no reason to be poor. I remember Bob Proctor once said, *"It is a sin to be poor"*. Indeed it is. When the universe is so grand, so much in abundance, why do we insist to stay poor through our thinking process? This should not happen. Because the Universe is Abundance itself, we are a part of the abundant Universe. There is enough for everyone. All we have to do is just call forth what we already have, in the spiritual realm, to physical manifestation. Always remember, we are whole and complete spiritual beings undergoing a human experience. Contentment is the key.

> *"Food is considered God, as it is the source of a person's life, body, mind, and character. Eat only what you need. Do not be greedy and take more than you can eat and waste the rest. Wasting food is a great sin; your surplus can feed another stomach. Even a major part of the food you consume, the gross part, is thrown out as waste matter. A minute amount of the food, which is the subtle part, is assimilated by the body and flows as blood. And*

a minuscule amount, which is the subtlest part of the food, makes up your mind. Therefore mind is the reflection of the food consumed. When demonic tendencies arise in our minds, know that it is from the food we consume. To receive real nourishment, pay attention to the quality of food that you eat and let it be very pure, clean, sanctified, and Satwik."

—Sri Sathya Sai Baba

CHAPTER 6

A WORLD WITHOUT GUNS

"Your vision will become clear only when you look into your heart. Who looks outside, dreams; who looks inside, awakens."

—Carl Jung

Carl Gustav Jung—psychiatrist & psychotherapist

Let us see how man has lived so far. Let us have a brief overview of the current situation on our planet. Man has made great advances and technological breakthroughs in the field of science. The invention of the light bulb was indeed the turning point in the history of mankind. It paved the path for greater and greater inventions and discoveries in relationship to man and his surroundings. Ever since Rutherford split the atom in the early part of the twentieth century, there was no turning back. Science has virtually reshaped the way we live our lives. The inventions of the last fifty years have marked the beginning of man's escalation to greater and greater discoveries of himself and the universe at large. The marvels of modern medicine have made the blind to see, the deaf to hear and the lame to walk. Those who were born without limbs or those who lost them due to an accident or a disease, can now have limbs. Today we can hear of those who are not so fortunate achieving the impossible feats, like mountain climbing and taking part in races with prosthesis. Those who cannot talk can communicate through a word synthesizer, those who are paralyzed are able to move around with the aid of special equipments. Many diseases are also kept at bay with the discovery of more and more modern drugs. These have in a way prolonged the human lives.

From the engineering aspect, man has not only made vehicles to travel at incredible speed on land but also into space and in the sea. The automobile industry has made leaps and bounds in their area of development from the days of Henry Ford, and today we have fascinating vehicles with superb shapes and models, some running on fossil fuel, some on bio-fuel and some on solar energy. Man has also conquered the sea through the invention of huge vessels that not only travel on the surface of the water but also beneath the sea. Giant container carriers cross the oceans on a daily basis, carrying goods from one country to another with ease. Under water cameras has made deep sea diving and travel a very interesting chapter in the lives of man. He is now able to understand sea creatures and vegetation at the bottom of the sea with ease. A voyage to the bottom of the sea is just a piece of cake, unlike before. Unsatisfied with the conquering of the land and sea, man decided to look up to the sky, and asked himself, what is beyond the clouds. Copernicus and Galileo Galilee will be in a state of disbelief should they find out what their initial attempts in astronomy have turned out to be. The advances in the field of astronomy have been simply astronomical and the achievements and discoveries are still ongoing. It is simply marvelous. Man has not only managed to locate new moons on Jupiter, new planets and new universes but has made rockets, able to cruise the space at unimaginable speed and at the same time send photos of our Universe, back to planet Earth. He has not only put man on the moon, but also satellites in space. Everyday new discoveries are made which adds as new chapters to this field of science. It is simply amazing. These momentous discoveries in the world of science should be a celebration of one of humankind's greatest technological achievements. In spite of all these advancements of modern man, man has not delve into the most inner recesses of his mind to enquire as to why he is behaving so ruthlessly and aggressively as he is doing so thus bringing about much misery not only to himself but to the whole of mankind. If that can be done, man would come to a realization that he, as an individual is responsible for the collective. As an individual, he is contributing to the violence of the world, as long as he has not addressed the issues bothering his mind. The totality of the human psyche is also known as the Collective Unconscious, a term of analytical psychology, coined by Carl Jung. It is proposed to be a part of the unconscious mind, expressed in humanity all life forms with nervous systems, and describes how the structure of the psyche autonomously organizes experience. Jung distinguished the collective unconscious from the personal unconscious, in that the personal unconscious is a personal reservoir of experience unique to each individual, while the collective unconscious collects and organizes those personal experiences in a similar way with each member of a particular species.

If only man, as a race, instead of running from one philosophy to another, one religion to another, searching for ways and means to escape from ourselves, but seeks clarity, an understanding of the actual state of mind, a new man will be born. And that is because a new mind has been born, not a dull mind, a troubled mind or an old mind with all the memories of miseries and misfortunes attached to it. It will now be a free mind, with great energy, razor sharp capabilities with penetrative powers which will see things as they are. We will never disregard another human being again, their feelings and their lives. We will seek to respect and honor them as how we would like to be treated. But when one is faced with such a momentous task of bringing order in the structure of a society where there is so much to be done, he will be overwhelmed with the issue so much so that he will resign to the fact that there is nothing much he can do, or just very little. There he stops. But the problem requires a much deeper answer.

Guns and bombs are not dangerous, if left alone. They can be triggered only by man. World peace is indeed a personal matter. We need a change in consciousness, not circumstances. The new world order will see no guns around. All nuclear warheads will be dismantled. All guns will be melted in the furnaces. All forms of artillery and arsenals shall be destroyed. This will be an outcome of the understanding of the concept of Oneness. Man shall have only one 'weapon', and that shall be the weapon of love. Why do we need to go on creating more and more of weapons and build up our arsenals? Whom are we going to fight with? Aliens? The aliens could be laughing at us. They think we are insane. We are doing something we don't like and yet we go on doing it. We are killing our own brethrens. This has to be stopped.

> *"If we could establish a deep abiding relationship with nature we would never kill an animal for our appetite, we would never harm, vivisect, a monkey, a dog, a guinea pig for our benefit. But apparently man loves to kill things, the fleeting deer, the marvelous gazelle and the great elephant. We love to kill each other. This killing of other human beings has never stopped throughout the history of man's life on this earth. If we could, and*

we must, establish a deep long abiding relationship with nature, with the actual trees, the bushes, the flowers, the grass and the fast moving clouds, then we would never slaughter another human being for any reason whatsoever. Organized murder is war, and though we demonstrate against a particular war, the nuclear, or any other kind of war, we have never demonstrated against war. We have never said that to kill another human being is the greatest sin on earth."

—J.Krishnamurti

Imagine a world without destructive weapons—whether of mass destruction or not, is not the question. But this step will be a giant step in the history of mankind. For man to take this bold and giant step, he has to eliminate fear and distrust. This brotherhood of man has to be built on trust and love. The trust that another nation will not invade another country, in pursuit of that country's riches and bountifulness. What is the purpose? These are the very act of domination that has created the present miserable situation where trust has no place. The present world is running on the idea of "might is right". This is a very primitive way of thinking. Apparently we have not evolved far from our ancestors in our thinking although we have advanced very far in terms of technologies. All our discoveries and rich cultural heritages should and must never be gone to waste. We have come a long way, let us preserve them. Let us pre-serve life itself instead of serving our selfish needs first.

People have a wide spectrum of mentality. We have humans from the very crude type of thinking to the very refined mentality. Then we have humans who are cunning and want to have power over others. The uneducated can be educated but the cunning ones are the problematic ones. These are the trouble causers. They are the greedy ones who are capable of running the underworld. And they can be very powerful. Certain countries are virtually run by these kinds of people. So the difficulty lies in showing these people the way of love. They wouldn't miss an opportunity should they be given half a chance to raise their ugly head of greed and superiority. The nations cannot disarm as long as these types of people are in existence. For them, might is still right. Compassion and love are for mere weaklings. But can we at least start by dismantling all our nuclear heads first. And I mean *all* of them. No one country should be allowed to own even one. When this is achieved, we can say that a giant step towards the goal has been established. These would take a lot of trust among the countries who have the capability to develop nuclear bombs. One big headache has been taken care of. Next cut the annual budget for military expansion drastically. We don't need any expansion on these areas at all. Expansion for what? It is real waste of public and government funds. This money, which may amount to billions of dollars annually, may well be channeled to feed the majority of the population of the world. Most of them in many countries go to bed hungry every night.

> *"The world is a dangerous place to live; not because of the people who are evil, but because of the people who don't do anything about it."*

> —Albert Einstein

The New World Order will not come to effect if we are stuck in the old mindsets. We must be serious in coming anew in every situation. The Universe is waiting in eagerness to respond to our actions. Remember, we have to come from Love and treat everyone alike. Just have a look at the article below, entitled, *'The Last Post'*, which I received from a friend of mine via email. This would render our hearts soft and show all of us the utter futility and madness of war.

'The Last Post'

If any of you have ever been to a military funeral in which The Last Post was played; this brings out a new meaning of it. Here is something everyone should know. We have all heard the haunting song, *'The Last Post.'* It's the song that gives us the lump in our throats and usually tears in our eyes. But do you know the story behind the song? If not, I think you will be interested to find out about its humble beginnings.

Reportedly, it all began in 1862 during the American Civil War, when Union Army Captain Robert Ellicombe was with his men near Harrison's Landing in Virginia. The Confederate Army was on the other side of the narrow strip of land. During the night, Captain Ellicombe heard the moans of a soldier who lay severely wounded on the field. Not knowing if it was a Union or Confederate soldier, the Captain decided to risk his life and bring the stricken man back for medical attention.

Crawling on his stomach through the gunfire, the Captain reached the stricken soldier and began pulling him towards his encampment. When the Captain finally reached his own lines, he discovered it was actually a Confederate soldier, but the soldier was dead. The Captain lit a lantern and suddenly caught his breath and went numb with shock. In the dim light, he saw the face of the soldier. It was his own son. The boy had been studying music in the South when the war broke out. Without telling his father, the boy enlisted in the Confederate Army.

The following morning, heartbroken, the father asked permission of his superiors to give his son a full military burial, despite his enemy status.

His request was only partially granted. The Captain had asked if he could have a group of Army band members play a funeral dirge for his son at the funeral. The request was turned down since the soldier was a Confederate. But out of respect, they did say that they could give him only one musician. The Captain chose a bugler. He asked the bugler to play a series of musical notes he had found on a piece of paper in the pocket of the dead youth's uniform. This wish was granted. The haunting melody, we now know as 'The Last Post', used at military funerals was born. The words are:

Day is done. Gone the sun.
From the lakes From the hills.
From the sky. All is well.
Safely rest.
God is nigh.
Fading light. Dims the sight.
And a star. Gems the sky.
Gleaming bright. From afar.
Drawing nigh. Falls the night.
Thanks and praise. For our days.
Neath the sun, Neath the stars.
Neath the sky 'As we go.
This we know.
God is nigh

CHAPTER 7

MEDITATION
&
HEALING MODALITIES

"As a broken microphone cannot broadcast a message, so a restless mind cannot transmit prayers to God."

-Sri Sri Yogananda Paramahansa

Sri Sri Yogananda Paramahansa
Founder of Self Realization Fellowship

The purpose of meditation is not to show off to others that you have certain powers and thus a much better person than another. Should that be the case and the reason to do meditation, then I suggest that you don't start off at all in the first place. The sole purpose of meditation is *a soul purpose*. It is to establish balance and harmony in one's self, physically, emotionally and mentally which would eventually give rise to the realization of one's true self. It helps an individual to be in the present moment, the Now, that which is timeless, that is before any thought processes. This is where silence is. This is where stillness is. And in this silence and stillness, you will find the beauty and the magnificence of Life.

The practice of meditation on a daily basis will help an individual rise into higher and higher realms of awareness, thus discovering greater truths about himself and one's connection with nature. It will also help an individual to come wholly from himself rather than from one aspect when dealing with others. This will make his relationships 'holy' because he /she is coming as a whole being and not as an un-whole being in the dealing with the world. This is to say that one is *mindful* of his intentions. He is utilizing his whole mind. And the mind is not just in the brain but in every cell of the body. The brain just happen to have more cells than any other organ, so people tend to think that the brain is the mind. It is not. The brain is the processer. It runs the body. It is a very delicate and complex electrical component, which will make our computers look like toys by sheer comparison.

Meditation can be an instrument to bring about a new you and a new me as many have been engaged in it for some have discovered for themselves. It is a technique to help you strip yourself of all the layers of illusion in which you have clothed yourself through ignorance. Meditation, as many would imagine, is to sit silently at a particular place at a particular time in a particular position, focusing the mind on a single object for concentration. This can be a starting point for beginners but meditation is far from just that.

Meditation is not a state of the body but that of the mind. Meditation is something that cannot be taught because it is something that *happens* when all the right conditions are met. What can be taught about meditation are only techniques. What happens after that in the individual's mind, the teacher has no control over it. For example, we can till a plot of land and plant a seed in it. We can water it and guard it from all kinds of dangers, and that is the best we can do, but we can never force germination of the seed to take place. As to when the germination of the seeds will take place, no one knows. It is the same with meditation. No one can tell when meditation takes place but it is important to prepare the mind for it to happen. And when it happens, you and only you will know and hence derive the benefits there from.

Meditation of the mind can be a source of medication for the body, as how world renowned author, Norman Vincent Peale would put it. Calming the mind has a very positive effect in creating a stress-free body. A body that is free from stress will have a high level of immunity against viruses and bacteria. This will therefore bring about a healthy body, fit to carry out the daily activities of our lives. And that is the only physical instrument we have to do all other works. Without a healthy body, nothing is possible to achieve.

> *"To begin to establish right relationship with human beings, not the everlasting battle between sexes, between human beings, killing each other, terrorizing each other, destroying the earth and so on, so on, if we don't stop that, what is the good of your meditation? Meditation is Giving Thought its Right Place"*

> *-J.Krishnamurti*

There are many techniques in meditation and the practitioner ought to find the best technique suitable to one's temperament. Not all techniques are suitable for everyone. Here, I would like to share with you two simple techniques which can easily be practiced. Do this regularly so that this ritual can focus your attention and your intention. Always stay in the richness of the Now. Moment to moment. This inner richness will be expressed externally. Everything will fall into place. This sense of richness will bring about a feeling of contentment, and this is the greatest wealth you can ever have. Then you have actually tapped into the inner reservoir of abundance, the never depleting source of true wealth.

MEDITATION ON THE HEART SUTRA
by Deepak Chopra

Dr. Deepak Chopra

Author, holistic health and alternative medicine practitioner

Go to a quiet place where you are not likely to be disturbed for fifteen minutes. Close your eyes, practice the primordial sound mantra, ie. "so-hum" for five minutes, placing your awareness on your breath. After five minutes, put your mental awareness in the area of your heart, in the middle of the chest. With your attention on your heart, you may begin to feel your heart beating more strongly. This is normal.

As you experience the beating of your heart, begin to also experience gratitude.

The way to experience gratitude is to think of all the things, events and relationships in your life for which you have reason to be grateful. Allow these images to surface in your consciousness while you keep your attention on your heart. Take a moment to think of all the people whom you love and all the people who shared their love with you. Then, say to yourself:—"Every decision I make is a choice between a grievance and a miracle. I let go of grievances and choose miracles".

Certain resentments and grievances and the people associated with those resentment may surface in your awareness. If they do, just say, "I let go of the grievances. I choose the miracles". Then become aware of your heart again and consciously start to breath into your heart. As you do, say to yourself, "love, knowingness, bliss, love" and then breathe out for the same count of four. Between each inhalation and exhalation, pause for several seconds. Do this for three or four times. The fire of your soul which is love, knowingness and bliss, will start to broadcast itself through the heart. The fire at your soul now begins to create your intention. The Heart Sutra teaches, "form is emptiness and emptiness is form" The Heart Sutra advises the practice of deep meditation to gain wisdom and enlightenment and the realization of the emptiness of form, feeling, perceptions, volitions and consciousness.—Deepak Chopra

AWARENESS ON BREATHING

The second technique which I would like to share with you is the meditation technique where we put our awareness on the inhalation and the exhalation of our breaths. Just be aware of your breathing in and your breathing out. You can do this anywhere. It is not necessary that you have to be seated in a comfortable chair. Of course it can be done that way too. The best part is, this technique can be done just anywhere, be it whether you are travelling in the train, or in the bus, or even while waiting for the bus to come. You can do this while in the car, waiting for the traffic lights to turn green. You can do this while waiting for your fiancée to come by. You can do it while waiting for your meal to arrive in a restaurant or waiting in a queue in the bank. It is so simple yet practical. You will not feel that time is wasted. You will be utilizing your time to the maximum. You can do this with your eyes open and it can be done very inconspicuously, without having to draw other people's attention. You can even do it while walking in the woods or in the park, lying down on the bench. The best part is your tension with other people will diminish a great deal. As there is no more waiting for anyone or anything. This is an excellent technique for anyone suffering from insomnia. When you lie down to sleep, do this technique. In a very short while, you will be dozing off. You have to try it out to believe it.

The method of doing it is very simple. One inhalation and one exhalation is called one breath. Five inhalations and five exhalations is called one *kriya*. Ten *kriyas* would be called one cycle. So to complete one cycle, it should not take you more than ten minutes. And as we inhale and exhale, bring the awareness to the breathing process. Be aware that you are breathing in and be aware that you are breathing out. And as you breathe, do not force breathe. It should be light and natural like the normal breathing. When this technique is done over a period of time, on a regular basis, you will come to a state of mind which is very sharp. It can detect even the slightest movement of emotions in your body, which you were not able to do so before. With this kind of clarity, you will be more focused in your daily activities and things get done with much ease and with less effort and struggling. This technique helps us to stay in the present moment more often than not.

The science behind this technique is that breaths represent Life itself. Some of us may think that we are breathing. If we are breathing on our own will, then we should be able to control our breaths anytime, and we know jolly well that we cannot. You can only stop breathing for a few seconds or a minute or two only. That is the maximum. It doesn't take a genius to find that out. In reality we are *being* 'breathed in and breathed out.' Our lungs are acting like a bellow. The rhythm of the universe makes this so. So breath is Life itself. It is life energy. Some call it the God energy. Whatever you choose to call it, it keeps you alive and rejuvenated. So by being aware of our breaths, by being mindful of our breathing process, we are keeping a very close contact with God or Life. Both are synonymous by the way. We are filled with positive energy, and that will keep our cells healthy and active, and our mind alert. Both are needed with sharpness and agility to carry out our daily activities with optimum results. This is because we are spending more and more time in the sacred moment of 'now.' This is the place of happenings.

In the days of The New World Order, man would have come to a realization that yesterday and tomorrow are but figments of the imagination of man. *Now* is the only time there is. When we stray away from the present, holy sacred moment of Now, we will be caught in the net of delusion. Then, suffering sets in and our world will be in turmoil again. Meditation will be part of the school curriculum and early training in the psychic arts will follow. Young children will be encouraged to get in touch with their "sixth sense" and to train, use and expand their psychic power. Thoughts must exist for our lives to function. Inwardly thought breeds pain, sorrow and a constant drive for pleasure brings its own frustrations, disappointments, anger, and jealousy. It is important to exercise thoughts only when it is necessary, and the rest of the time observe & look. The old thoughts that prevents the actual experience of looking will drop away. It will be possible to live totally in the moment of 'now'. Meditation is something everyone should strive to do, whether they are young or old. It is more important that very busy people spend a few minutes a day in meditation. If you cannot spend even five minutes for meditation because of your work load, *it is more the reason that you should embark into the process of meditation.*

Now that we are on the subject of meditation, I cannot but help discuss a bit about healing, the healing of both the mind and body. There are many healing modalities available but here I would like to share with you three of the most powerful techniques of healing that I know of and where I have experimented with. One such technique points to the ancient method of healing employed by the Hawaiians. This technique is called Ho' Oponopono. This powerful technique was made popular by a Hawaiian doctor named Dr. Ihaleakala Hew Len in the treatment of hardcore criminals who have been declared as beyond any redemption.

HO'OPONOPONO

> *"The only task in your life and mine is the restoration of our identities, our minds, back to their original state of void or zero."*
>
> -Dr. Ihaleakala Hew Len, Phd.

The healing method of Ho' Oponopono is based on the principle that there is only One Mind. There is no such thing as my mind and your mind, thus creating a perspective of many minds, perhaps 7 billion minds. Since there is only one mind, then the problems faced by my fellow brothers and sisters in their minds have to be my problem as well. So the problems have to be in my mind. And therefore it has to be my problems as well. This reinforces the point I was trying to drive home before, that is "We Are All One."

Going by this understanding and operating from this premise, Dr Hew Len brought about an astounding miracle in the lives of some hardcore insane criminals. Let's have a look at this astounding miracle.

THE MIRACLE OF HO' OPONOPONO

Dr Hew Len worked for about four years in a special ward in the Hawaii State hospital where people who had committed extremely serious crimes like murder, rape, kidnapping, etc. were imprisoned. They were there because of deep and serious mental disorder or they needed to be checked to see if they were sane enough to stand trial. Apparently the staffs working in that ward were working there rather unwillingly and most of them rather take off and stay away from their work, because of the fear of being attacked and the negative vibrations they were being exposed to. They rather be on sick leave than being confronted by these criminals. Even though the inmates were shackled all the time, because of their relentless threatening attitudes, they would not be brought outside to get some fresh air. That was the situation of the ward then. It was reported that even the paint on the walls would peel off and new paint would not even stick to the walls.

Such was the repulsive state of the ward. Dr. Hew Len cured the entire ward of criminally insane patients without ever meeting any of them or even spending a moment in the same room, where previously many other doctors have failed miserably. He healed them by healing himself. He never tried to see them personally. Just by going through the records of each and every insane patient, he healed the entire ward, by using the technique of *Ho'oponopono*, or Dr.Hew Len's updated version known as Self I-Dentity. He says, *"The only task in your life and mine is the restoration of our identities, our minds, back to their original state of void or zero."*

Eventually things began to improve little by little in the surroundings. The environment became more palatable. Paintings of the walls were possible. Some of the prisoners would not be shackled anymore or would receive less pharmacological drugs. Gradually, more and more of the prisoners managed to obtain permission to go outside, to get fresh air, unshackled, without causing trouble to the hospital staffs. Over a period of four years where Dr.Hew Len spent there, prisoners were released gradually except for a couple of inmates who were relocated to somewhere else, and eventually the clinic for the mentally insane criminals was closed down.

It is important to note that both reconciliation and forgiveness are very essential in any healing modalities for the healing to be effective and permanent. In the *Ho' Oponopono* technique of healing, the method of reconciliation and forgiveness, is based on four simple steps. They are:

1. I am sorry
2. Please forgive me
3. I love you
4. Thank you

REIKI

Another healing technique which I am involved as a practitioner is known as *Reiki,* whose founder is a Japanese doctor by the name of Dr.Mikao Usui. *Reiki* was discovered in the 19th century in Japan, and was made popular in the West by one of his close students, Mrs. Takata.

Dr.Mikao Usui—Founder of Reiki

The Science & Philosophy of Reiki.

Reiki, a Japanese term, literally means 'Universal Life Energy. It is holistic system of healing discovered by Dr.Mikao Usui. It treats the whole body, physical, mental, emotional and spiritual. It can be used to channel life energy into your body, which will improve our immune system, thus restoring health. But reiki is not only used for the sick. You need not be ill to use reiki. Regular application and practice of reiki on oneself can on the long run remove whatever mental blocks there may be, thus paving a new way of viewing life and circumstances of life. It is a life changing phenomenon. It can bring an individual to heightened awareness, harmony and spiritual growth through its regular practice and application, eventually leading one to enlightenment.

Reiki is a simple, natural and safe method of spiritual healing and self-improvement that everyone can use. It has been effective in helping virtually every known illness and malady and always creates a beneficial effect. It also works in conjunction with all other medical or therapeutic techniques to relieve side effects and promote recovery.

This technique involves twelve hands-on positions over the various parts of the body where the seven major chakras are located. The constant use of this method helps to repair and rejuvenate the chakras, which could have been damaged, or they could be in a state of over-functioning or even under use. The seven major chakras has direct connection with our autonomous nervous system, which are linked to our endocrine system, which is responsible for the healthy functioning of all our major organs of the human body. When the energies are not flowing smoothly as it should in the meridians of the body, due to blockages, the body is said to be out of balance, which would eventually result in sicknesses and diseases.

Before the practitioner begins the healing process into motions, he or she is expected to recite the five precepts namely:

1. Just for today, I will not anger.
2. Just for today, I will not worry.

3. Just for today, I will do my work honestly.
4. Just for today, I will respect all lives.
5. Just for today, I will count my blessings.

Reiki practitioners will come to know that there are basically three levels of learning in Reiki, namely Level 1, Level 2 and the Master Level. At Level 1, you will be exposed to the 12 hand positions, while in Level 2, you will be introduced into certain symbols which can be used for the healing purpose, even for distance healings. In Level 3, you will be introduced to more symbols and you will be taught the techniques of initiating others into Level 1 and 2. For more information and in-depth knowledge, you may visit www.reiki.org.

THE HEALING CODES

The third technique of healing that I have been involved as a practitioner is known as The Healing Codes, founded by psychologist Dr. Alexander Loyd.

Dr. Alexander Loyd—Founder of The Healing Codes.

The Science & Philosophy of The Healing Codes

The basic concept of the Healing Codes method is that all memory is stored as pictures, and these pictures have non-truths or lies in them which, if left uncorrected, eventually result in emotional and/or physical disease. When these pictures are healed, the stress related to these pictures and events will also be released, thus enabling the immune system to kick in again and heal the body of its illnesses back to health. Activation of The Healing Codes on oneself removes the underlying stress and impact the unhealed pictures of the heart. It is said that illness and disease can be traced to an unhealthy energy frequency. If you can change the unhealthy frequency to a healthy one, the illness or disease would go away without drugs, surgery, counseling, or even effort. And many ways to change "unhealthy" frequencies to "healthy" frequencies had already been discovered and validated—and one was so powerful it literally had a healing effect on human DNA.

With the application of the Healing Codes, Dr.Alex discovered that his clients' feedbacks saw that they not only healed the spiritual and emotional issues that were targeted but surprisingly many also saw the disappearance of physiological disorders that they have not even discussed. Unexpectedly, the Codes were addressing the whole person. This has happened despite the fact that they have never targeted any disease or any physical problem. The only issues that were targeted are destructive, unhealed memories that are stored as pictures in the heart, because these are the source of stress.

Pierce Howard, PhD, author of *"The Owner's Manual for the Brain"*, says that data is encoded into us in the form of images. Rich Glenn, PhD, in his book, *"Transformation"*, states that "the disruption in the body's energy system can be traced to a disruptive picture, and the replacement of that picture creates a permanent healing effect."

Their conclusion is: Destructive images which are often unconscious, causes both physical and non-physical illnesses.

So what makes the picture so destructive?

According to quantum physics, everything is energy at its most basic level, and everything is in a state of vibration and has a frequency that is transmitted to whatever surrounds it. The energy that emanates from painful, negative memories and the cells that contain it, is unhealthy for the cells. Just as cancer cells are a result of these destructive frequencies, negative emotions and unhealthy beliefs are the result of the destructive frequencies produced by negative and painful images. The Healing Codes work because of established laws of nature in the field of quantum physics.

Any frequency can be changed if we only know how to do so. It uses unseen energy to remove unknown and unseen things that may be causing harm to people. Those unknown and unseen things are called *"pictures of the heart"*. In short, The Healing Codes, when applied correctly, activates a physical function built into the body by God, or by nature that consistently and predictably removes the number one cause of illness and disease from the body, and that is stress.

According to Centers for Disease Control and Prevention in Atlanta (CDC), Stanford University Medical School, and numerous health experts the number one killer on the planet is stress. Most physical and non-physical health problems have long-term physiological stress as their origin. And 80% of all health care dollars are spent on illness related to stress.

Cellular biologist, Dr. Bruce Lipton's research at Stanford University indicated that over 95% of all illness occurs because of stress in the body's autonomic nervous system. Deeply held wrong beliefs about our circumstances and our selves are the causes for such stress build-ups in our system. We learn wrong beliefs in several ways. Most of them are from negative experiences, from our parents, our teachers and our peers. We even inherit them in our DNA! There is even evidence that genetic diseases originate because stress damaged the genes of our ancestors. Wrong interpretation of our circumstances causes unhealthy activation of what is known as the "fight-or-flight" syndrome which has three components.

1) The autonomic nervous system triggers the pumping of adrenalin into our bodies so that we can run faster or fight harder, literally to survive the current situation.

2) Resources including blood flow, nutrients, waste removals and oxygenation—are shifted away from our internal organs, immune system, and higher intellectual functions, and shifted to large muscle groups and brain stem, where reactive thinking occurs.

3) Individual cells receive an alarm message from the nervous system to shift out of growth and into the self-protection mode.

And cells in self-protection mode are susceptible to illness and disease; whilst cells in growth mode are impervious to illness and disease. The body was designed to go into fight-or-flight mode only when our lives are threatened, and then immediately go back to growth mode when the threat has ended. If the body stays in this state long enough, illness and disease are likely to follow. This is the process that creates 95% of disease & illness.

Instead of killing viruses and bacteria, the Healing Codes targets memories related to the issue a person is thinking about. Using positive healing energy frequencies, it cancels out and replaces the negative, destructive frequencies. Healing energy has transformed destructive energy that was stored as cellular memories in the body, ultimately affecting the physiology of the cells in the body.

The validity of The Healing Codes is established by the client's reports of self-healing from all manner of problems, including many regarded as incurable. Mainstream diagnostic tests also showed that stress was consistently removed from the body following the use of a Healing Code. (Heart Rate Variability). The Healing Codes seems to work almost 100% of the time. At a conference in Mexico, 142 out of 142 who did a Healing Code on a memory related to the biggest issue of their lives had the negative power of that memory healed down to zero or 1 on a 10 point scale. For more information on The Healing Codes, a book has been authored by Dr.Alexander Loyd which goes by the same title.

You may surf the webpage www.thehealingcodes.com and you will have an in-depth knowledge of this method of healing.

In addition to the above three techniques which I have described, of course there are many more healing modalities, but I am not in a position to comment on them as I have not been involved in them. Some of them are yoga, traditional counseling, thought field therapy (TFT), emotional freedom techniques (EFT), Healing Touch, Tapas Acupressure Technique (TAT), Quantum Techniques and many others.

Whatever techniques of healing you may be engaged with, affirmations too can play an important part in enhancing the healing process, provided there isn't any conscious conflict with your conscious mind. Your conscious mind must be able to accept the affirmations as the truth or else it will reject it outright and the reciting of it will be just a waste of time or may even make matters worse, as now you have introduced something else for your mind to tackle and to get rid of. One of the best ways to make an affirmation work for you would be to implant that affirmation into your sub-conscious mind at a very relaxed state. And you are most relaxed when you are about to doze off to sleep and when you are just about to wake up in the morning. During both these times, your brain wave activity would be at the Alpha state, that is, the electrical activity of your brain is at a frequency of 8.0—13.9 Hz. and it can be measured using an electroencephalograph machine, also known as an EEG. Alternatively, you can get into a relaxed state of mind through the meditation techniques that I have mentioned earlier or relaxation music which is easily available on the internet.

Over the years of self healing, I have come up with my own powerful affirmations and they have powerful impact on me, and my sub-conscious mind. Whatever we put into our sub-conscious mind will have an effect in our daily lives. So it pays to pay special attention as to what you are putting into your mind on a regular basis. As far as possible, being in a positive state of mind, reading positive materials, mixing with positive people will definitely produce positive outcomes in your lives. Some of the positive affirmations that I would like to share with the readers are as follows.

> **I am abundance itself. Abundance is my birthright. I am ever connected to the Universal Life Energy all the time. I am always complete and whole. I am never in need of anything and I have no wants. Everything I ever want or need is already here. The energy, the stuff that all things are made of, physical or non-physical, is already here, all around me, within me all the time. There is *never a moment* that I am not with this energy, this ever creative energy. There is *never a moment* that I should despair or worry. For such a state of mind is non-benevolent.**

It is a negative state of mind. Such a state of mind creates only negative situations in life.

I need nothing to be happy. Happiness is a state of mind, a higher mind. The lower mind or the egoist mind is forever looking for problems, for situations to fix, so as to make known its presence, its existence. It wants to continue to exist.

I am whole and perfect. I am at peace and at ease all the time. I am always joyous and happy. I am powerful, radiant and strong. I am ever expanding and ever present all the time. I am most of all, loving and caring. I care for all people and all living and non-living things. I am a good steward of my environment.

I am one with God. I am God. I am whole, perfect, strong, powerful, loving, harmonious and happy all the time. Death of the body is no matter to me, for I continue to *be*, in eternity. Life situations are easily solved, for nothing is impossible for me.

I am Divine and I always live in the ever presence of my divinity. I am at all times sensitive to the feelings of the people around me. I am ever watchful of my thoughts, words and my actions, lest I may offend someone. The darkness of my lower mind disappears the moment I recognize or become mindful of my divine nature.

No problem or life situation is impossible to solve, no matter how knotty it can be. It is all a matter of being present in the moment of Now. The deeper I am in the Now, the easier I can access my infinite power and the problem solves by itself, almost effortlessly.

My thoughts are well guarded and I am careful not to emit negative or destructive thoughts. I make it a point to emit only positive, benevolent and wholesome thoughts all the time.

"We cannot solve our problems with the same thinking we used when we created them."

—Albert Einstein

CHAPTER 8

PARENTING
&
THE EDUCATION SYSTEM

"Be the change you want to see in this world"

-Mahatma Gandhi

Mahatma Gandhi—nationalist, spiritual leader and an advocate of non-violence.

In the days of the New World Order, there will be no more room for carelessness nor will we leave the important affairs of man to chance. Man will give his attention to all affairs of his life, especially in the affairs of the younger generations, like parenting and education. It is a big surprise that such a very important task of parenting is not a subject in school curriculum. There is not even a small introduction even at the pre-university level. So young people who suddenly end up as parents are not really ready, at least psychologically, to meet the immense responsibility that they are confronted with. Unable to cope with the situation, many opt for divorce. So single parents are created to make matters worse. In some case, none of the young parents would want to take responsibility for the new born. So the baby may just end up in a bay hatch if it is lucky. For those who are not so lucky, they may end up in a cardboard box placed at someone's door. Orphans are created. Unwanted teenage pregnancies and baby dumping has been a very serious issue in developing countries. Some babies have ended up even in commodes! This cannot and must not go on.

Parenting will be considered the most important part of all activities. The parents will remember at all times that the little ones are looking at them for directions, with their mouths wide open, wondering what to say, what to do, how to respond in any given situation. Parents themselves will be their first role models before their teachers. Not only both the parents but also the immediate family members especially the elders and also the community. The little ones will not be looked upon as outsiders but as family members too. This is because, in the days of the New World Order, man would have expanded their vision of the way they see the community. It will no longer be a localized family unit but an integrated one. The elders will play a very important role because of their wisdom acquired through their longer time lived on earth. The younger energetic parents, who are still learners themselves, as they have not experienced much of life, may not be the ideal parents just yet. This is where the elders come in. The young parents will have more time to discover themselves and also learn from their parents.

Compared to now where both parents go to work to earn money to pay for their expenses, in the days of the New World Order, this need not be so. When the rat race has come to an end, there will not be an urge anymore in them to 'keep up with the Jones'. Only one parent will work. The other will ensure that the environment where the child is exposed to is safe for his growth. Safe in the sense that it is all conducive and healthy for the healthy development of all the faculties of the child's various domains. The mother will be the better candidate for this job. She, having been the one who bore the child for nine months, breast fed it, and caressed it the most, the child will have a natural affinity to the mother than the father. The responsibility of upbringing the child will be the most important agenda in their lives.

Pouring out love through their words and actions will make the child realize at an early stage of his or her life that every affair shall be based on Love. He will grow up to be mindful of the utterance of his words and his actions, not only to his fellow human beings but also to the animals and the environment around him. Love for the planet will come naturally to him. There would be no necessity for worldwide campaigns to create public awareness on this matter. There will be no wastage of public funds. From their home the children are taught these values. Parents too will realize that aggression need not be way to solve problems. Violence has not and will not solve anything. Children of the New World Order will not know of violence as we know of now.

Televisions and computers, which play major roles in molding the development of the children, will play different roles all together. Stark naked violence that we approve now on the television and the cinemas, will be denounced and such programs will not be supported. Hence their demands will drop and sooner or later will cease to exist. This will not be just an ideal. This will be indeed the way of life. Actors and actresses will be paid for the promotion of rich values and cultures. They too will play in important role in human affairs, like the politicians. They will always bear in mind the consequences of their actions and the impact on the young minds. In short everyone is responsible for the bringing forth and the maintenance of the New World Order.

Love and care shall be the order of the day. The roles of immediate family members will reinforce the idea of love and non-violence in the young minds. The grandparents, who are much older and wiser, through their experience of going through the mill, will act as bulwarks during the impressionable period of the child's life. Their wisdom shall be second to none. They will impart their wisdom through their gentle touch and soothing voice. After all they too have been parents before. The other immediate family members too will be mindful of the presence of little ones. As a result, everyone changes their mode of behavior because they have seen enough of the present ways of living. They would have come to realize how their thoughts and actions can impact the world over. This will be a major breakthrough in the affairs of human lives. Children will be taught principles of love, kindness, honesty, respect and responsibility in their homes *first* even before they start going to school. Can you imagine what a big difference that will make in the school?

The big burden which the parents have now placed on the poor teachers will be lifted and for once the teachers can enjoy their profession, that is, teaching, not parenting. Once they enjoy doing their job, we can never predict what teachers are capable of. They can and will help to reinforce the values in their daily curriculum with ease.

Aggressive and confrontational ways of resolving issues will be something of the past. All will be done through discussion and matured communication with each others. This will apply to other areas like commerce, and politics as well. So the teachers will compliment the work of the parents in establishing the character of the child. When the beauty of the character in the child starts to bloom and blossom, there will be beauty everywhere. Parents and teachers will work hand in hand, all for the sake of the younger generation and the generations to come.

As said before, the New World Order will be based on brotherly love. There will be no room for greed, hatred and selfishness. We will not distinguish our children from other people's children. Those selfish ways of thinking and mentality will not work. We will embrace the child of another as our own and shall take responsibility for its welfare. The idea of Oneness will be made a reality, not just a mere slogan. This is how we will create the New World Order.

"Children are living beings, more living than grown up people who have built shells of habit around themselves. Therefore it is absolutely necessary for their mental health and development that they should not have mere schools for their lessons, but a world whose guiding spirit is personal love."

-Rabindranath Tagore

Rabindranath Tagore—Poet

In the days of The New World Order, the method of teaching will vary a great deal compared to what is being done today. Our education system of today can be considered as the most boring and the most unenthusiastic way of teaching. What we now call education is merely accumulating knowledge from books. Such education offers a subtle form of escape from ourselves and creates increasing misery. Conflict and confusion result from our own wrong relationship with people and things. Until we understand that relationship and alter it, the gathering of facts and the acquiring of various skills, can only lead us to more chaos and destruction.

Though we produce many scholars who pass their examinations in flying colors and distinctions, very little has been done in the production of real human beings. What our schools, colleges and universities are producing are more like humanoids, quite robotic in nature. They are not taught how to think creatively but instead they are taught what to think according to certain syllabus determined by the government of the day. The students are fed more and more of knowledge, immaterial whether the knowledge is the truth, a lie or even half-truths. They are taught to memorize them and fill in the blanks during an examination. This is utter rubbish. This is not called education. This is called rote learning. There is very little or no encouragement to question the authenticity of the given subject. As the government changes every four or five years, the education systems also changes. This seems to be quite the pattern in many parts of the world. We seem to be fooling around with the most important issue of a human being and also that of the nation. This is observed to be true even in the teaching of the religions to the young ones. We are required to simply accept whatever is forced down our throats. This explains why most students are bored to death and find other avenues for their excitement.

In the days of The New World Order, the education system will be an inspiring one. How would that be? Unlike now, the students will be given as little information as possible about a particular subject and they will be required to explore, investigate and come to their own conclusions. They will be encouraged to think freely and question openly, without fear or favor. Students will be encouraged to be open-minded and view the world from a broader perspective, unlike now. Interference from parents in the education system will be brought down to a minimum, if possible, none at all. The teachers are fully responsible once their children are in school and parents should respect the teachers and the school administration to do their job. There ought to be trust in the wisdom of the teachers and the system.

With regards to the syllabus, in addition to the current subjects, there will be extra emphasis in the teaching methodology and the subject matter. They will be made more value based. Value based education will ensure that the students will imbibe a good character in addition to the secular knowledge, which is important to earn a living. A good character will ensure that the student will know how to relate to another in a harmonious and respectable manner, which would not in any way cause another to lose his peace and hence result in disharmony. It is very vital for all nations to produce young people with sterling character as they will be the future parents and future leaders of the world.

In the days of The New World Order, relationships will be of utmost importance and all dealings will be based on truth, trust and brotherly love. Any attempt to cheat another will not be entertained. People will shun dishonesty. Students will be taught principles in honesty, truthfulness, love and kindness in their school main syllabus, perhaps integrated with their main curriculum. Only when there is beauty in character, peace and harmony in the homes can be ensured. When there is peace and harmony in all the homes of all the nations, there will be peace in the world. So we can see that world peace is truly an individual matter. Michael Jackson couldn't be more accurate than this when he sang the song, *"Man In the Mirror"*. Our hope for the realization of the New World Order is in the young ones. Let us not forsake them and the future of this beautiful planet, just because of our sheer greed and insanity.

> *"Good parents give their children Roots and Wings. Roots to know where home is, wings to fly away and exercise what's been taught them."*

> —Jonas Salk

Right education is a mutual task demanding patience, consideration and affection. In the days of The New World Order, education will be a different ball game altogether. It will be a value based education system unlike now where students are fed with information, which could be half-truths or even lies. Students will be encouraged to think freely and critical thinking will endow them with the necessary wisdom for a harmonious and a fruitful life. It is vital that the relationship between the teacher and the student be a strong bond based on the principles of love and understanding. The same teacher will have to continue to be the mentor during the early impressionable years of the students. Changing teachers every now and then would leave the students without a mentor. This would leave them vulnerable to undesirable forces.

CHAPTER 9
RACE & RELIGIONS

"Let the different faiths exist.

Let them flourish and let the glory of God be sung in all the languages and in a variety of tunes. That should be the ideal.

Respect the differences between the faiths and recognize them as valid as long as they do not extinguish the flame of unity"

—Sri Sathya Sai Baba.

Sri Sathya Sai Baba—*The Avatar of the Modern Age*

We do not know how we came into being. Some religions say that God created the Universe. Scientists say the universe is a result of the Big Bang. Whatever the case it may be, how we have come into being is not as important as how we *live* it. Many people are of the opinion that the world is in a very bad shape today. It could partly due to the information that they are being constantly fed by the mass media. Newspapers and television stations are so profit orientated that they are willing to sensationalize any news as long as the readership increases which subsequently would roll in mega bucks for the companies.

There are lots of good events happening in the world that goes unreported. Lots of positive information that would actually help man to view the world from a different perspective which would allay fear from his minds but sadly, man is inundated with much negative information. As a result many are of the opinion that the world is on the path of self extinction. The fear of a nuclear holocaust is real, no doubt, looking at the arms race we are having today, to show who is mightier than the other, to show who is superior than the other, and all it takes is one psychopath politician to get the fireballs rolling. Our rich cultures, traditions, languages, arts, architectures, music, science and technology are threatened to extinction.

But this type of thinking cannot be helped especially so when we have religious bigots who goes around proclaiming the greatness of their own religion while at the same time denouncing the other religions as if they are lies. They proclaim that their particular religion is the only true religion. The others are at best some poor substitutes. Religious and spiritual chauvinism has played a big role in creating much negativity in the minds of men. It is indeed surprising because they are suppose to be doing quite the opposite, ie. elevating man to a higher consciousness where oneness is prevalent.

Of course we cannot deny that there are genuine people with noble intentions in all the religions and they too are trying their best to unify mankind under one banner of brotherhood. Unfortunately, the editors of the newspapers and the television stations do not think this is important and sensational enough to make their sales skyrocketing. They thrive on disunity of the people. With these types of negative reports, many would want the existing religions to become defunct and extinct from the surface of the earth as soon as possible as they appear to be a bane to mankind. They have caused much pain, heartaches and suffering, and misunderstandings among fellow human beings. Currently our intolerance towards the religions of our fellow human beings has brought about great despair and animosity.

Religious tolerance is such a negative phrase. This is as clear as daylight and yet most of us are not willing to see and think and act differently. This cannot and must not go on. This will bring more and more ruins onto ourselves. In the days of the New World Order, the challenge facing all the religionists is to sit on a common platform and scrutinize their religious books, together. Bring out to the open the great common truths that all these great religions have to say. There is no room at all for religious chauvinism for we have seen that it breeds hatred, anger and disunity. Wars have been fought and nations have fallen, millions have perished. It is not worth it at all. Life is much more precious than to be sacrificed at the altar of religious bigotry.

Religions will play a very positive role in the lives of man if and only if the religious leaders can have the courage to separate themselves from the power crazy politicians, whose sole intention is to wield power over the people, making them their pawns in their political game of chess. Religious leaders have a very great responsibility and an important role in forging out a united brotherhood of man, by highlighting the strengths and the goodness in each and every religion. It is in there. The Great Masters cannot be wrong. They spoke great truths, all for the benefit of mankind and not for a particular race of people. Christianity is not just for Christians and Islam is not just for the Muslims and Buddhism is not just for the Buddhist and Hinduism is not just for the Hindus. They are for all mankind. There are common truths. Why focus on the differences which separate man from man when we can focus on the similarities which can unite mankind? It is simple logic. The idea of *my religion is more superior than your religion* will be something of the past in the days of the New World Order. It is rather a very primitive way of thinking.

The days of glad tidings are at hand. It all depends on us, more so on the religious leaders and their courage to stand up for the common truth. There is much more that we do not understand about Life, about Nature, about God, for which once understood, will make a huge difference in the lives of all mankind. The fundamental question is, "Are we willing to make that move for greater and in-depth understanding and accept the fact that the ocean of the unknown is far, far greater than what is known by our limited mind." When this door of willingness is open, we will be opening our hearts and minds to the creation of a new way of living, we will be opening up to usher in the Golden Age.

"There is only One religion; the religion of Love,
There is only One language; the language of the Heart,
There is only One race; the race of Humanity,
There is only One law; the law of Karma,
There is only One God; He is Omnipresent."

Sri Sathya Sai Baba.

CHAPTER 10

POLITICS OF THE NEW WORLD ORDER

"I have a dream that my four children will one day live in a nation where they will not be judged by the color of their skin, but by the content of their character."

—Martin Luther King, Jr.

Rev. Martin Luther King, Jr.—pastor, activist, humanitarian and leader in the African-American Civil Rights Movement.

How would the political climate be in the days of the New World Order? Very simply, equal justice, good governance and fairness will be the pillars of support of the politics of the day. In all fairness to everyone justice will be served, fairly and proportionately, in accordance to the gravity of the "mistake" done. It is a mistake because man has not come to understand many things about his life yet. In the process of living, he may commit certain actions which may not be acceptable to others, maybe harmful.

There will not be any form of punishment where he will be deprived of his one and only life as we now practice in some countries till even today, known as mandatory death sentence through lethal injections, by hanging till death or burying a person's body in the ground up to his neck and stoning him to death or even cutting off limbs as a form of punishment. Man would have come a long way from this type of mentality, which is considered barbaric in some countries. When we come to a realization that we are indeed a part of them and they are a part of us, we are actually collectively responsible for the creation of the "criminal" and the 'crime' as well. Our present collective consciousness is a fertile environment for the development and growth of social problems. They will strive very well because we are actually fertilizing the environment for their growth, by our thoughts and thought patterns.

At all times we have to remember our thoughts have the power to impact the world over. Today, man is enveloped and wrapped all over by a consciousness of sadness, sorrow, anger and hatred. So punishing another has become a norm. We are acting from existing energy levels of anger and hatred which affects the human psyche very easily. That is why it is so important to come anew in every situation and ask ourselves whether we want to re-enact our past by reacting to a particular situation or do we want to create a new situation, by coming from our reservoir of love. Did I not say that we are all brothers and sisters in one big family? Would we want to kill our brother for a 'mistake' he has committed or shall we, through our brotherly love, show him the correct path? He must have been driven to do what he did out of anger, frustration, depression, suppression, oppression or from sheer greed for money due to difficult situations in his family life or just plain greediness. Whatever the reasons maybe, he can be taught the way of love. No one does anything wrong, given the model of the world he holds in his mind.

In the days of the New World Order, governance of people will be kept to the minimum. This is because man would have come to a level of maturity where he will be able to self-govern himself. The responsibility will not be placed on the heads of the politicians as it is now. There will be so little of governance of the people by the politicians. At that time it will truly be a *'government of the people, for the people, by the people'.* It would then have become a living reality. That would be the politics of the New World Order.

Today, most politicians are afraid of losing power. At any cost they will want to stay at where they are. Even if it means being in power through the illegitimate ways, by assassinating his opponents, by throwing his opponents into jail, by creating trumped up charges, by cheating during elections by manipulating the votes, by threatening the election commission, by buying votes of the people through bribery and all sorts of other methods which he can think of. As a last resort, they may even incite hatred among the people through their propaganda and start a revolution so that a state of emergency can be declared and seize power over the people by force.

The current political scenarios around the world is not very encouraging. People are been suppressed. In every direction they turn, they are stifled. In certain countries, politicians have combined their religious teachings to run the country. This has further trapped man. In short man has become a prisoner of his government and his religion. Freedom of speech and freedom of expressions are not allowed, or even if it is allowed, only to a certain limit. The people are not allowed to highlight the shortcomings of their political leaders because they consider themselves above the law. Those in power can siphon billions of dollars and enrich themselves and their family members and they can still go scot free. In short, corrupt practices by the Executive can infiltrate into the Judiciary and as a result, we find that injustice is being served instead of justice, all just to keep themselves in power.

In the days of the New World Order, we will not be hoarding. We will not be grabbing and causing others to be deprived and leave them to suffer in silence, until they cannot continue to do so, which as a result, they would then protest and revolt. Politicians and religionists in particular, do not want any form of revolution as this will tarnish their "good" image. So they will, at any cost, try to suppress those who revolt and speak up. They do not realize that this is the people's way of expressing their discontent, and that they cannot take it anymore. Those who revolt are telling the politicians to stop immediately what they are doing. Change what they are doing. But those who are drunk with power will not heed those calls. They want power *over* the people. In the New World Order, this will not happen. The power will be *with* the people, shared with the people. Equal Justice shall be served to one and all, not to those in power only. In the days of the New World Order, our politics will be of a different ball game. Politicians will not run their opponents in the mud anymore. They would have realized their sole purpose of being in politics, ie. to share their power with the people by serving them, and giving people back to themselves, their dignity and self-respect.

CHAPTER 11
BACK FROM THE FUTURE

"I have come to light the lamp of Love in your hearts, to see that it shines day by day with added luster. I have not come on behalf of any exclusive religion. I have not come on a mission of publicity for a sect or creed or cause, nor have I come to collect followers for a doctrine. I have no plan to attract disciples or devotees into my fold or any fold. I have come to tell you of this unitary faith, this spiritual principle, this path of Love, this virtue of Love, this duty of Love, this obligation of Love."

Sri Sathya Sai Baba

Neale Donald Walsch—*Author of Conversation With God*

Those of you who are familiar with the *'Conversation With God'* series of books authored by Neale Donald Walsch would have come to realize by now that there is a Higher Mind, a Higher Consciousness, which is always in communion with each and every one of us. This Higher Consciousness, which he termed it as God, is not limited to a selected few, but to all of us. Many of us do not realize this as a reality simply because they believe that it is too good to be true. As a matter of fact, Neale Donald Walsch encourages us to communicate with God all the time.

So I too decided to do *'neale donald walsch'* session one day with my guru, my spiritual teacher, whom millions around the world revered and have accepted him to be an Avatar, an incarnation of God in human form. He is none other than

Bhagavan Sri Sathya Sai Baba, who resided in Prashanti Nilayam, Puttarpati, India, whom I addresses Him as Swami.

"A unique being, an extraordinary Man arises in this world, for the benefit of the many, for the happiness of the many, out of compassion for the world, for the good, benefit and happiness of gods and men. Who is this Unique Being? It is the Tathagata, the Exalted, Fully Enlightened One."— Anguttara Nikaya Pt.1, XIII P.22 (Buddhist Canon)

(One evening, as I was relaxing and idling away on the easy chair lying on the porch of my house, sipping away some BOH Tea which we bought during our recent trip to Cameron Highlands, listening to the birds chirping away perched on the *bunga kemuning* tree in my garden, embracing the gentle wind blowing on my face, I could smell the sweet fragrance of the *bunga kemuning*, which happened to bloom on that day. The next thing I knew was I had gone on a truly beautiful journey with my beloved Bhagavan Sri Sathya Sai Baba.)

Come! Let's go.

Where to, Swami?

To a place called Earth.

But we *are* on Earth!

I know. We are going to visit your future.

My future?

Not yours! The future of mankind.

Wow! That's fantastic. Something like a time-tunnel? I enjoyed that TV serial very much.

Well, it's something like that but we will not be going through any tunnels this time.

This is exciting man!

Can you see that distant blue planet? That's where we are going to. Doesn't it look beautiful from here?

Oh! Yes.

(And in a nanosecond, we had neared the planet and it was a scenic view. And we were hovering over and looking at the greeneries, the mountains, the rivers and the blue seas. It was such a panoramic view to behold.)

Well, it does look like our planet Earth alright. I have seen such pictures taken from the satellites in the internet.

You seem to be surfing the internet very often. Even some prohibited sites too. Naughty boy.

But it would be more beneficial to surf your inner-net.

It is an excellent medium, Swami. I get my work done with ease through the internet. It's much faster and more efficient.

But it cut both ways. We have to use our wisdom in using it. Many are abusing it to slander people and break up families.

That's true. Very true. I was such a victim.

Okay, now we are going to zoom closer and circle the globe and have a look at Earth from a much closer position. Look at the rivers, all the rivers. Look at the seas. Look how clean and crystal clear they are. They are not black or muddy or oily anymore. There is no silt moving in them. Can you see the dolphins skipping away merrily?

But Swami, how can this be? Most of our rivers and seas are known to be dead, or dying due to pollution caused by man. Man has been dumping all kinds of waste chemicals, mercury, plastic bags and bottles, sofa sets, televisions, bicycles and whatever they want to get rid from their homes. I remember throwing a bag of flowers into the river in Taman Sri Muda after a Thursday *bhajan* many moons ago. I am also one of the culprits, you know?

I know, I know. But that is the past. As I said earlier, we are now in the future of mankind.

Holly Molly! I . . . I.. I am speechless, Swami. I am floored! I do not know what to say. Pray, tell me, how many years ahead are we from the present?

Well, we are about forty years into the future.

Forty Years!! Let me see . . . so it is around 2051.

Oh My God!

Yes, you can say that again.

Oh My God!

You are a real comedian, you know that, don't you?

I know, You have said that before. My classmates saw that comedian in me in the 80's.

Look at the trees. They have grown. Can you feel the abundance and richness of the oxygen level? Finally man has understood his co-existence with nature. Thanks to all the fine minds, the environmentalist and the volunteers who helped to hammer this vital point into the minds of the industrialists, economists and the politicians.

Yeah. It took a long time for them to grasp a simple idea. It's not that they do not know. It's sheer greed.

Come, let us go to India.

To Puttaparti?

No.

Then where?

Wait and see.

(And then, suddenly, like magic, we were in a strange place. I have never been here before)

Can you see that man over there in white?

Most Indians wear white Swami. Which one?

The one that is moving amidst the crowd. The one with long hair and beard.

Oh, okay. I see him. To me he appears like Jesus Christ. My God! He has really come. The *'second coming'* which every Christian was blabbering about.

Yes, He has come. And that's me. That is Prema Sai Baba.

(At that moment, that bearded man looked up in our direction and nodded with a gentle smile on his lips.

My jaws dropped.)

Prema Sai Baba? This is getting weirder and weirder . . . . I mean, is this for real?

Why are you doubting, son? He still has a lot of work to do. Much of the work has brought fruition as you have seen earlier. He has to usher in the Golden Age. Many people will be called forth for this grand mission as I have done so during my time on Earth. Much groundwork was done. Now is the time to build the mansion. Did I not say that there are many rooms in my mansion? There are rooms for each and everyone of you.

I am so excited Swami. Will I be called to be part of the divine plan?

Why do you ask? You are already part of the plan. Everyone is. Everyone is special. But no one is more special than another.

As much as this is causing me much excitement, there is a pertinent question bugging my mind. Can we clear that first before we go any further?

I know what you are going to ask.

You know?

Of course I do. I am God and I am in you. Anyway, shoot.

Why did you decide to drop your mortal coil earlier than what was predicted? Every one, and I mean every devotee of yours were expecting you to live till 96 years of age. I read that information in *Satyam Sivam Sunduram Part1*, authored by Professor Kasturi. You left all of us, just like that, at a drop of a hat. And then some smart alec comes around and tells us that you **actually** lived till 96 as predicted, according to the Hindu lunar calendar. But why talk about a Hindu calendar only after your Mahasamadhi? Nothing of that kind was ever hinted to us when you were physically around. To me it sounded like mere justifications. Why, Swami, why?

Not again . . .

What . . . what do mean by 'not again'?

Well, definitely this is not the first time you are asking this question, right?

All right, I admit that.

Listen. Does it really matter whether I lived till 76, 86, 96 or even 106 years? Does it? You must understand that it is not the body that matters. The body is subject to the natural laws, whether it is My body or your body or anybody's body. It is born, it ages, it decays, and is subjected to death. So it shouldn't come as a surprise. What is more important is, what I came to accomplish in this incarnation, it has been accomplished. With a frail body, my movement was limited. My agility was hampered.

But you said you can change the sky to the earth and the earth to the sky. Millions of devotees all around the world were praying that you will recover from the ailments afflicting Swami's health. But You decided otherwise.

It is true that I can change the sky to the earth and the earth to the sky. Never doubt that. But one thing I will never do is cure Myself of my ailments. As it is, much abuse has been thrown at Me. Either way I will be ridiculed. Not that the ridiculing has any effect on Me, but it will have effect on you and the devotees, because of their love for Me. If I cure Myself, then I will be asked why I am not curing the ailments of all the sick people. I will be branded as a selfish God. And when I chose not to cure myself, I am said to be a goner. I am a powerless God. Sai Baba is gone. He has no more powers. He is not God as He claims to be. He has all kinds of sicknesses. How can He be God?

Listen carefully son, no one is free from blame, and I mean no one. Lord Buddha Himself was accused of fathering a child with Chinca, who faked her pregnancy during His days to bring disrepute to Him. Of course it was unfounded, and the truth was exposed in public by the devas. There will be no end to this. And as to why I decided to leave on the day I left, let it be a mystery. God works in mysterious ways. Try not to unravel the secrets of the cosmos in a hurry or else the game will be over. The curtains will have to fall. I hope that will settle that question once and for all.

I will go along with your answer but it doesn't answer my question as to why you decided to leave us much earlier than predicted.

There we go again.

In circles.

And that's because life does go in circles, to make you remember what life has got to offer and what your real purpose here on earth is.

Okay, Swami, let's go on. What have you got to show me about man's future?

What do you want to know?

How about their politics? How do they govern the people and their countries?

Very interesting. It is very much unlike the politics of your time.

Really? What do you mean? Don't they drag their opponents in the mud anymore?

No they don't. It is totally different. Much of the laws existing during your time have become obsolete and defunct. They do not exist anymore. Man, as a race has truly evolved in their political games.

Imagine if there is only you on this planet, tell me who is going to govern you.

Why, of course it has to be me and only me.

Exactly, that's what I meant. Self governance is the best form of governance. Man has come of age to govern himself. Therefore much of policy and law making has been reduced. In fact there is only one of us all the time. Remember I often tell you, We are All One? The One individuated into the many. Man has come to realize this great truth.

Oh! Thanks God for that!

You are most welcome.

I remember the gutter politics that we are forced to live with. Whether you like it or not, that type of politics has become a way of life. The way the opponents are ostracized, mocked at, condemned, insulted, insinuated, the false allegations, the so-called accidental deaths, the sexual traps and the assassinations, just to demean and bring disrepute to them. All because of the craze to be in power. They are just drunk with power.

Gone are those days, My son. As we go along in our journey, you will see that man has the capability of restoring his pride and dignity as a human race. And he will.

The politicians has come to realize that it is not about having power over anybody but sharing power with others that will bring the highest good for the citizens of the countries.

It is not about how tall you can stand in front of the people but how low you can bend to serve them.

It is not about how much wealth you can hoard for yourself and your immediate family members by your positions and status, but it's about how much you can share and distribute the common wealth, so that one and all can experience richness and abundance.

It is not about throwing pittance to the poor and the neglected but it is about raising them up to your own level, restoring their self-respect and dignity.

It is not about having powerful weapons to kill your enemies and plunder your enemies land but it's about cutting down on arsenal build-up and enriching the poor nations.

Indeed there are no enemies. You have created them along the way.

Wow? That was an earful. I am so glad for the changes.

Well, you asked about the politics of the future, right? What else do you want to know?

Swami, how about the present day religions? Have they become extinct like the dinosaurs? I really, really hope they have. The organized religions have been nothing but a pain in my neck.

You seem to have an axe to grind against the religions, don't you?

As a matter of fact I do. I used to think that God has made a **big** mistake by giving mankind so many *different* religious teachers and different versions of Holy Books. So much damaged has been done in the name of religions. Wars have been fought and millions have perished. So much of negativity has been created in the human psyche, because of religions. Everyone claims that their religion is better than the others. I have people come up to me and say right onto my face that Islam is the best religion in the world. Then I have been to Buddhist seminars where I hear speakers mocking Christianity, Hinduism, the Confucius teachings and Islam, whacking them away till kingdom come. I have Hindus telling me that Hinduism is the mother of all the religions. I can hear the *imam* blaring out from the loudspeakers from the mosque near my house, calling all non-Muslims *kefirs* or infidels. I have Christians who come to my front gate and preach to me that all of us are going to eternal damnation in hell and will burn in the everlasting fires until and unless I embrace their Christian faith, and not just any sect but their particular sect, which happens to be better than the other Christian sects.

Swami, what I am trying to tell is, all these religious chauvinism and spiritual arrogance is not helping to elevate mankind in any way. It has created a vicious cycle and man is caught in it!

Wow! That was a mouthful.

I can go on and on. Then we have . . . .

Hold it! First and foremost, get this straight. God has not made a mistake for a long, long time.

And to answer your question about religions becoming extinct, much to your disappointment, it has indeed flourished as never before.

Holy cows!

Yes, indeed they are. Everything is holy, even the religions. The faults of the religions that you seem to be so worked up with, has nothing to do with the Masters and their Teachings. The Masters were crystal clear in their messages, no doubt about that. Along the way much changes has been introduced by those people in power, to suit their own whims and fancies, and people has misinterpreted some of the teachings according to their own understandings. However, that does not mean that religions are irrelevant anymore. The spiritual wisdom in them is very much alive. In the future of mankind, as you can see for yourself as we move into the communities now, you will come to see that man is rising to a common platform of true brotherhood. This is made possible through the unity of all faiths.

Unity of faiths? I always believed that this unity of faiths issue is a mere lip service. It is just a distant utopia. And you are telling me that it actually worked for man?

I am not only telling you, but I am also showing you. See for yourself how they live. Can you not see the true spirit of brotherhood? What you are seeing is only the beginning. To see it blossoming in full is the job of Prema Sai Baba, and believe me, I will succeed. There is no such thing as a failure.

How was this made possible?

Courage.

What do you mean?

Courageous spiritual leaders and lay people took the lead.

But they are the ones . . . .

Listen! Forget about what happened in the past. I am telling you what took place that brought about the realization of true brotherhood.

All right, I'm all ears.

Good!

Religious leaders, spiritual leaders and lay people saw the futility of all these exclusivist teachings and separatist doctrines, which were man-made. These teachings are not God made. God is all inclusive and encompassing, never exclusive. People began to see through their hypocrisy. These leaders agreed on common grounds, to filter and to sift, and hold onto the light all the teachings, and decided to do away with all those doctrines that were disuniting and exclusivist.

Amazing! This is simply amazing. Swami, I am sure such a unity would have brought about much upheavals in other areas of man's lives.

Oh yes, it has. Especially in the education of the young ones.

The most important sector of a society. And the authorities have been fooling around this issue for a long, long time.

Parenting and education are vital areas to focus on, for the development of a truly cultured and advanced society. There are no rooms for mistakes. Much have suffered due to misguided education systems which focus solely on rote learning and how to make a living. Not much emphasis was placed on how to live fully as a human being, in inter-relationship with his environment. The education system in the future of man has its focus on values, in addition to the now taught subjects like science, mathematics, geography, history and others. The values are integrated into the main school curriculum. The teachers become the role models or mentors for the children.

How about parenting? Will we see a change too?

Most definitely.

Parenting, like education, being vital areas for the complete development of the growing child, will be assigned to the people with experience in life.

I beg your pardon? You mean the children will be adopted by older people of the society?

Nothing of that kind. The raising of the children will be borne by the elders in the family and the community. They have gone through life and have the wisdom to be passed onto the younger ones. The ones who brought these little ones into this world are 'children' themselves. They have much to 'learn' and remember about life. But that does not mean that they are separated from their children. They will live together but the elders play more important roles than the parents themselves.

This is really interesting. That would mean families would live-in together, unlike now where the elders live all by themselves, while the young parents live separately and burdened to make a living and take care of their off-springs. The older ones are also taken care of. It is truly a beautiful way of living.

Of course it is. This is what is called community living. It has mutual benefits for one and all. The neighbors are part of your family and you are part of theirs. Their children are your children. There wouldn't be any form of segregation based on race and religious differences.

Oh Swami, I have always wanted to see people living like that, in peace and harmony. And to know that it has become a reality fills me with awe and happiness. Thank you Swami, thank you very much.

No, I must thank you and all the like minded people. You all made it happen.

I have no role in this.

Why do you belittle yourself? You just said that you have always wanted to see people living in peace and harmony. These thoughts are powerful. Don't underestimate them. When you have such noble thoughts you become an agent of change unknowingly. This will be added onto the collective unconscious, as what your Carl Jung speaks of. This will bring about amazing changes when critical mass is reached.

You mean, "*Be the change you want to see in the world*"?

Who said that?

Mahatma Gandhi.

Bingo! You are well read.

Well, not really. I know a bit here and there, that's all.

Do you always run yourself down like that?

I'm being modest here.

Be what you want but there's nothing to gain by belittling yourself.

Swami, let's talk about business in the future of man. Being in business myself, I would like to know how men do trade and commerce.

Come, follow me. Let us do some window shopping and you can see for yourself.

Window shopping with Swami!! In my wildest imagination. By the way, am I imagining all these?

What do you think?

I think I am imagining I am talking with you.

So be it. Are you ready to go shopping?

Now, look carefully and tell me what difference you see in the price tags.

There are two prices indicated.

Exactly. One is the cost price and the other is the selling price.

Then the customer would know how much profit the businessman is making. There is nothing to hide.

Of course there is nothing to hide. This is what transparency all about. There is no manipulation of figures to maximize your profits. Man would have moved out of the mindset that business is all about maximizing profits. Business is about offering a valuable service. The manner of doing business has totally changed and it is still changing for the better in large corporations and also in the banking sectors. They are becoming more and more service oriented and offer value for their money. It is very much unlike the business trends of your time where you manipulate figures to maximize your profits.

Well, I wouldn't call it manipulation. It is about *adjusting* figures to avoid losses caused by someone else's mistakes and misquotes.

You can say what you want. Manipulation or adjusting, it is still a dishonest act. You have done that in your own business as well, haven't you?

You are exposing me. And this is the second time.

No, I am not. I am being transparent here.

Thanks for the reminder. It really helps. You always have a way out, don't You?

Honesty will still be the best policy in the future of man. Honesty, responsibility and awareness will be subjects of the main school curriculum that you will teach your young ones.

This is unbelievable! That would really be a breakthrough in the evolution of man. It would be an evolution revolution.

Yes, it will indeed be. It will be a non-violent revolution, unlike many of the revolutions which man has seen in his history.

Man has come a long way, hasn't he?

Indeed he has. Man has matured. He has grown out of his growing pains, as how you would put it.

Is this the Golden Age which you have been speaking of?

Yes, but there is much more to achieve. The most difficult hurdles in raising the consciousness of man are over. The rest will just fall into place with little or no effort at all. Man truly deserve a New World Order, after all the sufferings and misfortunes that has befallen him.

How long will this Golden Age last?

Thousands of years.

How many thousands? One thousand? Two thousand? Five thousand?

Let that be a mystery to you. God works in mysterious ways. You have to love my uncertainty.

Swami, thank you so much for the glimpse of man's future. For a moment I thought we are going to lose everything we have worked for.

I love you, Swami, I love you.

I love you too. You know that, don't you? Have faith in Life, My son. As I said before man, as a species, is capable of reaching to the stars. Trust me, son, trust Me. I have faith in humanity.

Come, let's get back.

You are going off already?

No, your wife is bringing you another cup of tea. Please be gentle with her. She is also my child.

I am always gentle with her.

I know you better.

Excuse me, please!!